Peter N. Abbotts
29.11.81.

Reading and Spel

A m

Reading and Spelling Difficulties

A medical approach

Vera Quin and Alan MacAuslan

HODDER AND STOUGHTON

LONDON SYDNEY AUCKLAND TORONTO

British Library Cataloguing in Publication Data

Quin, Vera
Reading and spelling difficulties.
1. Learning disabilities
I. Title II. MacAuslan, Alan
362.7'95 LC4704

ISBN 0 340 25755 5 Unibook
First published 1981

Printed and bound in Great Britain for Hodder and Stoughton Educational, a division of Hodder and Stoughton Ltd, Mill Road, Dunton Green, Sevenoaks, Kent, by Biddles Ltd, Guildford, Surrey

Contents

Acknowledgments

The authors wish to acknowledge their indebtedness to the Research (Endowments) Committee of St Thomas' Hospital who made the existence of the Learning Disabilities Clinic possible by their generous support, and to Dr B.D.R. Wilson, Physician-in-Charge of the Paediatric Department and Dr E.A. Frommer, Consultant Child Psychiatrist, for their help and encouragement.

Thanks are due to Miss Jennifer Warner, formerly Senior Speech Therapist at St Thomas' Hospital, and to Miss Eva Carlson, the present Senior Speech Therapist, for their invaluable advice in the field of language development; to members of the Occupational Therapy Department who have contributed so much to the work of the Clinic; and to Miss Jean Hunt, Eurythmy Therapist, for her assistance.

There are a number of case histories quoted in the text; though the general picture presented of each is substantially accurate, details which would make the patients identifiable have been omitted and the names altered to preserve anonymity.

Where possible reference has been made to recognised authorities and a medical bibliography is provided at the end of the book.

The views expressed are based on the clinical experience of the authors and are essentially personal; if they are not in accord with those of the reader, it is to be hoped that they will at least provide grounds for thought.

The table on page 14 is taken from one in MCFIE, J. (1975) *Assessment of Organic Intellectual Impairment* (London: Academic Press), and Figures 1, 2, 3, 4, 6, and 7 are adapted from BROCKLEHURST, K. G. and WARD, H. (1958) *A General School Biology* (London: Hodder and Stoughton).

Figures

1
Introduction

If a child has an obvious defect such as severe deafness, cerebral palsy, or Down's disease (mongolism), the condition will be recognised at an early age, special help or schooling arranged, and adult expectation of academic achievement tempered accordingly. The children who attend for assessment at a hospital-based learning disabilities clinic have no such physical problems, but are those who do not succeed in class to the surprise of either their teachers, or their parents, or both. It is the job of the assessment unit to confirm that the child has a learning difficulty, then to identify any medical condition that may be related to the inability to learn, and finally to proffer advice based on findings. The most convenient yardstick for either learning difficulty or retardation is to compare the child's achievement in oracy and literacy with the average performance of children of the same age and intelligence. However, this fails to take into account general and individual circumstances. There are no tables from which can be read off the expected performance of a child, taking into account age, intelligence, social class, family size, language background and school experience, so that the identification of the learning disabled child depends on clinical rather than statistical evidence.

Medical interest is directed at the developmental, neurological and behavioural aspects of learning disabilities rather than at the lack of academic achievement.

Normal function is dependant on normal anatomical and physiological processes. The incorrect but often recited ability of Charles the First to walk and talk half an hour after his head was cut off serves to underline the need for an intact nervous system, essential if communication between humans by means of spoken or written language is not to be interrupted. Surveillance of a child's development in the pre-school years is the function of the doctor in his role as guardian of growth. Identification of disturbances of the neurological and other systems, and of any pathology causing them, is the interest of a large section of the medical profession, the prime object being to correct disorders before they have caused irreparable damage, or if possible to cure any underlying disease.

It has become apparent, both from epidemiological and individual evidence, that untoward events around birth can have an effect on the rate of development of the neurological system, which is peculiarly vulnerable at this time. The culprit is lack of oxygen, due to poor blood supply, prolonged labour, convulsions, or trauma. It may either reduce the number of brain cells, or limit the reservoir of supporting cells not yet fully developed, or hinder the insulation of nerve fibres. In its turn, defective insulation reduces the speed of transmission of some nerve impulses. There are no safe techniques for taking cell samples from the living brain, therefore information as to what is actually happening has to be gathered by less direct means. The principal investigatory weapons available are: the tracings of the electrical activity of the brain; scans; clinical examinations that evoke particular responses; tests of behaviour of the individual. Information from these may be compared with parallel information resulting from studies of large populations of children of the same age.

There is evidence that delays in development of motor skills, of co-ordination and of orientation, are associated with poor peri-natal histories and with learning problems, but that not all such children have these problems, and similarly that not all children with learning problems have poor birth histories. What is certain is that a lot of children with such minimal cerebral dysfunction have greater difficulty in developing at the same rate as better favoured children in the same circumstances, and that schooling is in consequence more likely to present them with difficulties. This is one of the reasons why the medical profession has entered a field which might be regarded as solely that of the teacher.

However, incoordination, unsteadiness on his pins, clumsiness and other minor delays in motor development are much less likely to be reasons for bringing a child to the doctor than unsatisfactory behaviour, unsatisfactory to the point of disrupting either the family or school life. Poor behaviour is the symptom which most commonly drives a family to seek advice; conversely an improvement in behaviour is the first and most easily recognised indication of successful treatment and management. Before parents label their child naughty, or teachers label him lazy, stupid, inattentive, disruptive or maladjusted it is important that some effort be made to find out why he is like that. Abnormal behaviour is a symptom, the cause of which must be identified before it can be tackled.

Teacher interest is directed at behavioural, developmental and educational factors and academic achievement is the chief visible sign of teacher success. A doctor's interest is directed at behavioural, developmental and neurological factors, normal development being the visible sign of medical success. Teachers' and doctors' interest overlaps; even where they do not, both have much to contribute to the other, and therefore should never work in opposition or isolation.

Identification and investigation of disturbances of learning require not only the link between teacher and doctor, being the generalists in this field, but also the advice and help of specialists such as the educational and clinical psychologists, speech therapists, audiometrists, remedial teachers and psychiatrists.

It is the purpose of this book to demonstrate some results of this link between the professions and the use which can be made of it to the benefit of the child, by describing the work of a hospital clinic and some of the conclusions drawn from that work. Case histories are given to illustrate clinical and teaching points. They are not there to prove that one type of therapy or teaching technique did or did not work in a particular case, but only to draw pictures of different conditions so that teachers may perhaps recognise similar children should they occur in their own classes. None of the little stories reaches a logical conclusion; they are not fairy tales in which attainment of a satisfactory reading age ensures that the Prince lives happily ever after. Life goes on after school, and tempting though it is to stop a story at the point most favourable to the reputation of the Clinic, it has not been possible to collect enough information from long-term follow-ups to present any valid figures. To give some basis for believing that the Clinic does some good, details of a number of cases followed up are given on pages 128-33.

Tests

Repeated mention of the results of two tests will be made throughout the following chapters: Intelligence Quotient (IQ) and Reading Age. The Intelligence Quotient is measured (by the clinical psychologist) on the *Wechsler Intelligence Scale for Children* (commonly abbreviated to WISC) and consists of a series of tests falling into two groups: verbal and performance. The verbal subtests investigate vocabulary, information, comprehension, auditory memory, and so on. Except for the optional subtest of auditory memory, they are to some extent dependent on the language of the home, education and reading ability. The scores of these subtests will be low if English is not the primary language of the home, or if the type of English spoken is not that in general use in the United Kingdom. Children who are poor readers may show a decrease in their scores as they get older and their loss of book knowledge and vocabulary becomes apparent. The performance tests measure the ability for abstract reasoning mainly on the basis of visual information. The whole test has not only predictive value, giving a reasonably accurate measure of a child's potential, but is also of great diagnostic significance, especially in the field of visual perceptual weaknesses. Discrepancies between the verbal and performance group scores are common. Marked differences usually indicate either some striking delay in language development, as has been mentioned earlier, or some degree of permanent change in brain function which will impair learning. Similarly a particularly low score in one or two subtests may also indicate a definable neurologically based deficit.

Wechsler classifies the degrees of intelligence like this: very superior,

superior, bright normal, average, dull normal, border line, mental defective. Fifty per cent of the population fall into the average range, which is a broad band of twenty points around the score of 100, scaled for age; each of the categories above and below this band represents another 10 points.

Reading Ages are measured by reference to tests which have been standardised on a normal population. The *Neale Analysis of Reading Ability* (an oral reading test) consists of passages graded for difficulty, each followed by comprehension questions. The Reading Age, or proficiency, of the particular child, is determined under three headings: accuracy, comprehension and rate of reading, which are related to the number of mistakes made, the number of questions accurately answered, and the number of seconds taken to read each passage. The silent reading tests, also timed, and the spelling tests, work on the same principles.

The results of these tests are not sacrosanct. They are a guide to the functioning of the child; the style of his performance and the type of response, both correct and mistaken, are of the greatest importance. A careful analysis of the reading mistakes in particular will give clues as to future remedial action. Close observation by several therapists may modify interpretation of results: is he trying to appear less proficient/younger/more distressed than he really is? How cooperative is he? A few 'Don't remember' or 'Dunno's will significantly depress scores in both the reading and verbal IQ tests. Conversely, the flattering one-to-one attention may draw out very good responses, particularly in the IQ subtests, where each question presents a limited and clearly explained task. Responsive children, who are 'difficult to settle to work' in the classroom often do almost misleadingly well in these test conditions. With such unsettled youngsters the tests are poor predictors of their ability to speak or argue, let alone write, to a theme, particularly in subject areas where success depends on selecting relevant detail from a much greater body of information. Children with long-term disease may produce poor results which improve startlingly when the illness is relieved and they feel well again; the improvement results not from teaching but from treatment of what may be quite simple conditions such as recurrent tonsillitis.

Limited as the tests are, their results are widely accepted — with a pinch of salt — and therefore all children who come to the Clinic at St Thomas' (and at the time of writing not far short of a thousand have been seen) are assessed by them.

It may be that the recently introduced British Ability Scales will supercede the WISC in Great Britain, as they have been standardised for a wide age range (2½ — 17) and provide the traditional features of the WISC and other similar tests. Speed of problem solving, reasoning, spatial imagery, perceptual matching, short term memory and basic scholastic achievement may be tested against expected norms. The Scales will aid the identification of specific problems and therefore the recognition of how to remedy them.

Anatomy of the Clinic

What actually happens in the Clinic? Each child spends two afternoons there for examination and tests. These are carried out by the Clinic staff, each member investigating different areas of functioning.

The *eurythmy therapist* looks into gross motor coordination, balance, orientation in space and the ability to reproduce rhythms, perform movements in sequence, carry out movements following verbal instructions. The Lincoln Oseretsky Test forms the basis of this assessment.

The *occupational therapist* identifies manipulative and handwriting skills and play capabilities, for as much learning takes place out of school as in it. She may also explore the visual perceptual development of the younger children, using the Frostig Test. This contains five subtests: eye-motor coordination, figure ground discrimination, form constancy, position in space and spatial relations. These terms are self-explanatory with the possible exception of figure ground discrimination which is in effect the assessment of a child's ability to spot a shape hidden in a confusing background, the penetration of simple camouflage. The test measures development in 'ages'.

The *speech therapist* investigates oral language, both receptive and expressive, auditory discrimination, auditory memory span, ability with auditory sequencing, articulation, tongue movement and mouth formation. These findings are supplemented by a routine audiometric test, and in some cases an additional speech audiogram is called for. If she feels the need to do so, she may use the more penetrating Illinois Test of Psychoinguistic Ability (ITPA). There are nine subtests in the ITPA, six of which deal with a subject's ability to cope with language symbols of conventional meaning whilst the other three explore his automatic sequential development by the 'non-meaningful use of symbols, principally their long-term retention and the short-term memory of symbol sequence' (McCarthy and Olson, 1964). Specific mention will be made in the text of the last of these subtests, that of short-term visual sequential memory. In this, the subject is shown increasing numbers of nonsense symbols etched on small tiles (they might be Scrabble pieces from the Far East) and asked to reproduce the order in which they are presented from immediate memory. Achievement is related to age.

The *teacher* tries to establish the extent of scholastic retardation: oral and silent reading, spelling, word recognition, phonic knowledge, and if necessary mental arithmetic, are tested.

The *doctor* obtains a family and medical history from the parents, and gives the child a medical examination which includes a vision test and test of visual sequential memory.

If no recent IQ is available the *clinical psychologist* administers the WISC test.

A solo task is the test of silent reading comprehension (the GAP and Gapadol tests are used, depending on age) and this is valuable for giving some indication of how a child tackles tasks without the constant interaction with adults. This is obviously an area of the greatest importance for scholastic achievement. It must be emphasised that while a child often achieves scholastically adequate scores under the stimulus of the adult's undivided attention, when left on his own he may be unable to cope. Being in undistracting surroundings is of little help even with the task made easy by being broken up into small units.

It is here that reports from school are of the highest importance. Unfortunately they are not always available: the parents may not wish the school to know that medical help is being sought; the school may disapprove of an outside agency being brought into matters considered to be solely the school's concern; the request for a report may not have reached the relevant teacher; time for writing it is invariably short. From 1981 it is hoped to make this task easier by increasing use of the Development of Reading and Related Resources (DORRS) assessment form, a remedial package for secondary pupils devised under the chairmanship of Dr M. C. Roe, Inner London Education Authority staff inspector for special education, and the Classroom Observation Procedure (COP) form for junior pupils, devised under the chairmanship of Mrs E. M. Hawkins, formerly ILEA consultant psychologist. Both will be valuable aids to the doctor, in the same way as the teacher's report is at present. For arguably the opinion of the teacher, who has had opportunities of observing the child over a period of months, is more likely to offer useful insights into the child's intellectual and social functioning than data obtained from tests and observations in clinical surroundings. Failing a teacher's report, some parents bring recent end of term school reports; exercise books are always asked for, for the younger children the 'reading book' is always enquired about, and sometimes also brought. Older ones are asked if any book is being read and discussed by the class as a whole.

In a hospital setting judgment is based in the first instance on the skeleton information provided by test results. This is fleshed out by the family and medical history, the various reports from the teacher, educational psychologist, educational welfare officer, social worker, general practitioner, and the observation of the child and his parents, severally and jointly, together with information given by each informally in conversation. Throughout the two sessions at the hospital every opportunity is taken to engage the child and parent in conversation, with the style of communication having as much attention focused on it as the content. In this context the secretary-receptionist's observations become very valuable, since she has had better and longer opportunities for watching child-parent interaction than the doctor or therapists.

Back-up from paediatricians, child psychiatrists, audiometrists, ophthalmologists and other specialist departments of the hospital is easily available, so that an accurate diagnosis may be sought.

The history of past events provides a Bayeux tapestry not only of the child's development but also of the ever-changing environment in which it has taken place. Untoward events occurring either directly to the child or indirectly in the environment may be of importance when considering possible causes of learning disabilities and therefore treatment and outlook for the future.

Adverse factors or untoward events

Untoward events, both biological and environmental, may occur before school age, but later on affect educational performance in apparently normal children attending school.

The list given below is admittedly incomplete since it is only intended as an index for the cases to be described in later chapters. It must be understood that it must not be used as a 'do-it-yourself' calculator for making a diagnosis in relation to a particular child. Many of the factors shown have not been proven to be certain causes of learning problems. However, more children having such factors in their histories will have difficulties than children without. A study of individual cases will show that it is quite possible to have experienced one or more of the events listed below, but to suffer no ill-effects in reading, writing, or other basic academic skill.

It must be emphasised again that the likelihood of some adverse consequence does not mean that it necessarily follows. Probability is not the same as inevitability.

Biological factors

Before birth — hereditary: these are suspected of being important but are not yet proven.

— intra uterine: maternal illness or absorption of toxic substances sometimes in the guise of medicines which may benefit the mother but not the foetus.

If occuring in the first three months, results are more

likely to be anatomical abnormalities than behavioural or psychological ones. If occurring later, motor, language or perceptual developmental delays may be apparent in the pre-school or school periods.

Birth and just after
— born too soon, too late.
— oxygen imbalance and disturbances of metabolism.
— physical trauma at birth.
— repeated infantile fits or convulsions.

All these may affect brain development with resulting clumsiness, delayed language acquisition before school, or a learning difficulty at school.

Pre-school
— repeated fits (the occasional fit associated with a fever is so common as to be unimportant in this context).
— trauma affecting the head: fractures of the skull or long periods of unconsciousness.
— infections of the brain or its linings.
— middle ear infections causing partial or intermittent deafness during the times when feedback or the cracking of the phonemic code are developing.
— psychiatric illness.

Environmental factors

A happy, stable family and home ensure a happy, stable child. Language development is of course dependent on the potential of the family in this respect.

Just after birth
— deprivation of maternal emotional and language environment, due to physical or emotional problems affecting the mother.

Pre-school
— family stress arising from parental discord, parental psychiatric illness, poverty.
— restriction of language environment due to competition with siblings.
— apparently normal events: moving house, death of relatives, birth of babies, parental absences.
— multiple languages in the home.
— overprotective parents.
— poverty, not so much financial, as of language, and of stimulating experience related to exploring physical environment.

In some cases the dominant factor and its effects may be obvious, in others one incident may create a situation which would be resolved if all else goes well, but which will be exacerbated by another seemingly unrelated event.

The cumulative effects of several relatively minor incidents may produce widening of the gap between expected and actual performance in later years. For example, a child born with a minor degree of neurological dysfunction due to birth trauma may be overactive and demanding from the very beginning. His needs may be easily satisfied by a mother for whom all is going smoothly, but if her emotional balance is disturbed by some outside occurrence, or if she has a large demanding family, she may not be able to provide all that he requires, though she would have been able to do so if he had been unaffected. Another child may have fits and the understandable anxiety of the parents may not be allayed by the medical profession; consequently they become overprotective and delay social development and the exploration of environment. Add a series of ear infections with periods of hearing loss, even minor ones, and a slight language delay is added to the picture, the whole making for a child who is able to manage at home but quite unable to manage at school.

Mild disturbances of neurological functions, poor behaviour resulting from them, fiercely competitive siblings, loss of language environment from hearing deficits, emotional upsets from death of hamsters, friends, grandparents, or departures of father on quite normal business leading to fears that mother may vanish too, can all sum to cause learning difficulties in the future.

The delay between the events and the obvious effects may be long, especially for sophisticated attainments such as essay writing, mathematics, or finding the way by aid of maps. The more demanding the task, the more the minor weakness is revealed; but its importance in life is dependant on expectation, which to a certain extent may itself be an adverse factor.

It is the large number of factors that are known to be relevant that necessitates investigation of each case by a team of specialists rather than by one. For the same reason, the term 'dyslexia' is useful if used to indicate a symptom which needs exploration. When used as a diagnosis it is not, for it may put a stop to the search for causes, which must be identified if effective treatment is to be instigated. When children come diagnosed as dyslexic, this frequently means that they have been examined by one specialist, teacher, psychologist, paediatrician, pyschiatrist, who has found nothing in his field to account for the learning difficulty. Full assessment by a multiple discipline team often reveals the likely cause and turns the erstwhile diagnosis into a symptom.

Thus the chapters that follow will not give a quick do-it-yourself diagnostic kit. The case histories will emphasise the contributions of the various members of the multidisciplinary team and reveal further layers of complexity which may point to possibilities of improvement or, just as often, limit severely the hopes of achieving any. The Clinic's function being diagnostic and advisory, suggesting courses of action is like the proverbial casting of bread upon the waters: some of it does not come back. Patients and their parents do not always tell us to what extent Clinic advice is followed. Some parents prefer not to press a school or other authority to implement Clinic recommendations. And even in cases where a measured improvement has been achieved and recorded (see the Epilogue on pages 127-33), it only pin-points the end of the child-Clinic interaction, one episode in the child's life. Learning disabilities persist into adult life, when with the wider opportunities open to the youngster such disabilities are circumvented rather than overcome.

2
Neurology

It is a mistake to bother about a child's underachievement at school and at the same time to ignore his brain. The mind cannot be divorced from the nervous system. A quick canter round the field of neurology will bring this home to anyone who thinks of 'nerves' as an unhappy emotional state rather than part of the anatomy.

What follows is the text of a lecture given to post-graduate students working for the diploma in special education. Readers with no interest in, or a proper knowledge of, neurology, are advised to move on to the section on epilepsy (page 18).

So, slice off the vault of the skull without damaging the tissues underneath and what do you see? An outsize walnut, the cerebrum, whose two halves, the cerebral hemispheres are patterned with deep fissures. If you could pick up the brain from the cup of the skull, you would find a stalk, the brain stem, running down to the spinal cord, and behind this, in the angle below the cerebrum, a fist-sized mass of nervous tissue, the cerebellum.

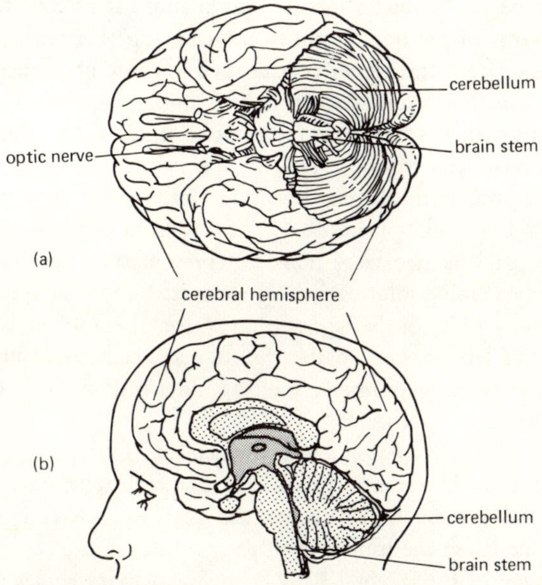

Figure 1 *The human brain: (a) — view from below; (b) — inside view of bisected brain. (In (b) cavities are stippled and cut surfaces are grey.)*

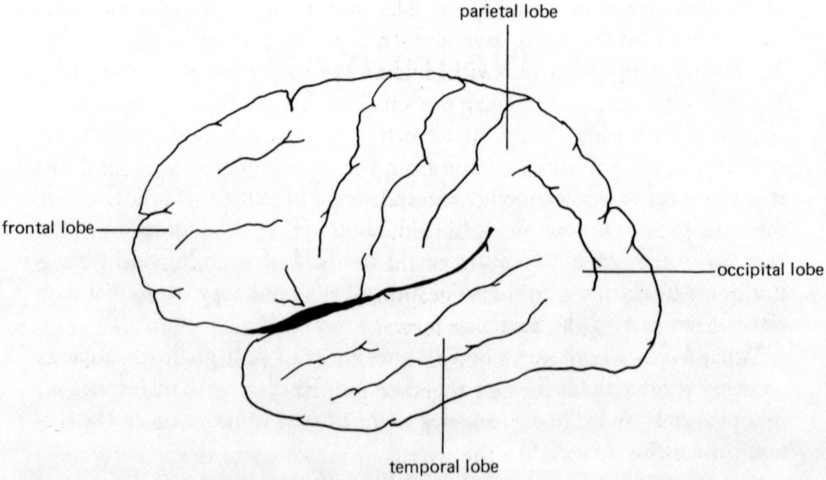

Figure 2 *Left side view of the human brain.*

The brain stem carries tracts of nerve fibres which relay impulses and messages to and from the periphery of the body to the rest of the brain. It contains those vital centres controlling breathing and the heart's action, without which we cannot live.

The cerebellum regulates muscle coordination. It receives information from the sense of position organs in muscles, together with instructions and messages from the higher centres such as those of balance, and puts the whole together in an orderly time and motion sequence. Consequently muscle movements take place in the right order, so that the pin can be picked up accurately from the floor or the staircase climbed.

The cerebrum is the largest structure. Its two hemispheres are connected by a thick white band carrying fibres from one side to the other; below the band lie two large masses of grey matter, the thalami, relay stations for incoming information. These exert a controlling influence on the tone and activity of the higher centres. Each hemisphere is composed of an external layer of grey matter, full of nerve cells, enclosing a core of white matter made up of interconnecting fibres running from one part of the hemisphere to another.

Anatomically each hemisphere is divided into four main lobes by the large fissures on the surface: the parietal, first seen when you peer down from above; the temporal just below this and just above the ear; the occipital at the back; the frontal in front.

Knowledge of the cerebral basis of mental activity comes from three main sources: the comparison of human with animal anatomy and function; observation of the effects of stimulation of the human cerebral cortex under local anaesthesia; the observed results of destruction of limited areas of the brain by disease and injury. The bulk of information comes from the study of adults, who have already acquired language and therefore must not be strictly equated with children who are in the process of so doing. It has been possible to map out small areas of the brain geographically, and relate various functions to each.

For example, incoming stimuli from the retinae of both eyes reach the receptor areas of the occipital cortices; damage to a small area of these will result in a blind spot in the visual field, because that blind spot is mirrored exactly in the damaged portion of the brain. If the damage occurs in a slightly different area, then the location of the blind spot changes too. If the injury occurs slightly further forward, no blind spot results but there is difficulty in seeing an object as a whole. Individual features may be recognised but cannot be put together properly. Luria quotes a patient who mistook an outline drawing of a pair of glasses for a bicycle, because he confused the lenses with the wheels. Stimulation of the receptor areas produces flashes of light or spots of colour in the patient's visual fields, as though he had been hit on the back of the head and was seeing stars; stimulation further forward results in hallucinations reflecting past visual experiences, and things seen are recognised for what they are.

McFie has summarised the functions impaired by damage in the other lobes of both cerebral hemispheres.

The question marks in relation to the right frontal lobe emphasise how much we still do not know about what really goes on inside ourselves. It has not yet been possible to attribute anatomical sites to all functions, and in particular efforts to identify the whereabouts of sites of complex ones such as thinking have not yet been very successful.

Extrapolation backwards in time from the adult to the child is tempting, but this is not a simple matter, for the developing brain is not the same as the developed brain. To some extent the differences are dependent on the stages in development of the microscopic systems.

The nervous tissues are made up of grey and white matter. Grey matter consists of small cells (glia) supporting the main nerve cells (neurons), each of which has a cell body (a mini-electrochemical power house) and one or more ultra-gossamer fibres branching from it. The long ones, called axons, may be several millimetres in length, are covered in an insulating sheath of myelin, make up the white matter and carry impulses from the cell body. There is only one axon to each cell. The short fibres, called dendrites, branch out like a small bush in winter, are not myelinated, make contact with axons from other cells, other dendrites and other cell bodies at junctions known as synapses, and carry impulses to their cell body. There is usually more than one dendrite to each cell.

Each axon ends in a bulb which contains bubbles (vesicles) and between the bulb and the receptor surface of the opposite dendrite there is a space

	Left Hemisphere			Right Hemisphere		
Level of Function	Frontal	Temporal	Parietal	Frontal	Temporal	Parictal
1. Sensori-motor	Right (and bilateral) limbs	Principally right ear	Right (and bilateral) sensory fields	Left limbs	Principally left ear	Left sensory fields
2. Integrated skills	Motor speech, writing and praxis*	Sensory speech	Ideational praxis,* Reading, Spelling; 'simultaneous' perception	?	Melody	Spatial perception in all modalities
3. Intellectual abilities	Verbal Fluency	Verbal Reasoning	Number Construction	Insight into errors?		Spatial ability
4. Memory	Verbal S-T	Verbal L-T	Verbal S-T and sequence	Visual non-verbal S-T	Visual (and auditory non-verbal) L-T	Visual non-verbal S-T and L-T

S-T, L-T = short-term (immediate), and long-term (recent), memory
*praxis = purposive motor control.

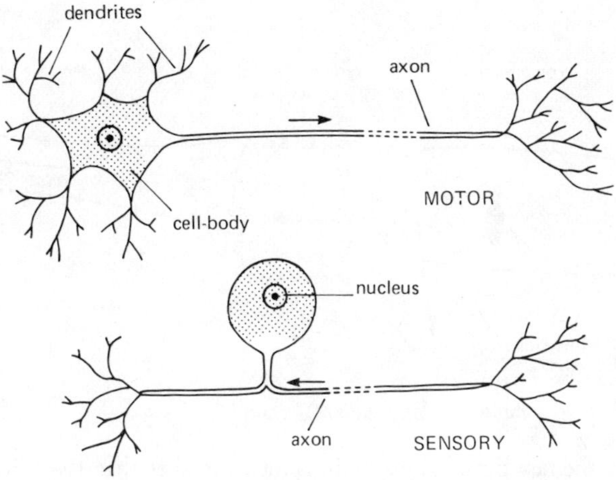

Figure 3 *Diagrams of a motor and a sensory neuron. (Myelin sheaths and the greater part of the axons are not shown.)*

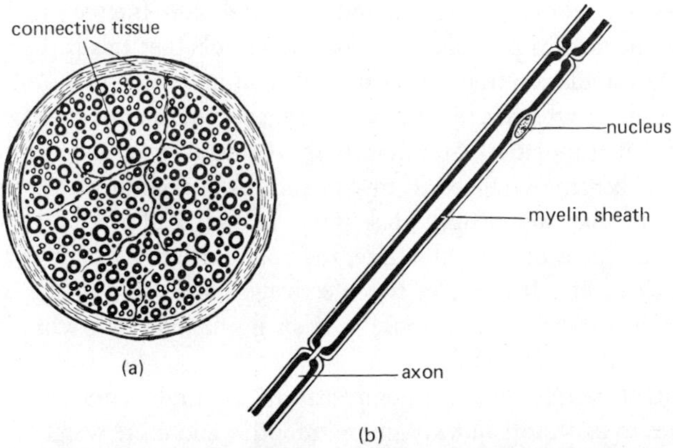

Figure 4 *(a) — diagrammatic transverse section of a small nerve; (b) — diagrammatic longitudinal section of part of a single nerve fibre.*

across which the biochemical transmission of impulses takes place. An impulse travelling down an axon to the bulb liberates an excitatory substance from the vesicles (bubbles), which then transfuses out of the axon, across the synaptial space, and latches on to the receptor of the next dendrite, starting a wave of excitation along its length to the cell body. Surplus excitatory substance is reabsorbed into the bulb, any backfiring up its own axon being prevented by a blocking system. Some medicines and poisons work on different stages of this synaptial transmission of impulses, either enhancing or suppressing it.

The formation of the neurons (main nerve cells) is more or less completed by the sixth month of foetal life, so that we are all born with the same number of cells as we should, all being well, have when adult.

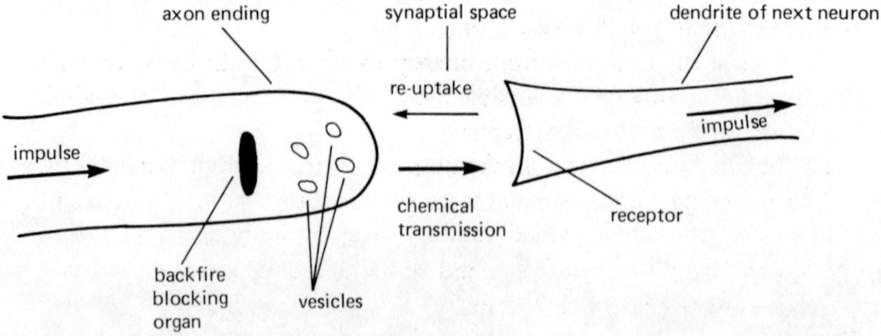

Figure 5 *A synapse — longitudinal section.*

However the newborn baby's brain is much smaller than the adult's, and quite a lot of growth has still to take place. Several different things happen. The processes of the nerve cells grow, so that more and more synapses (junctions) are formed, and more and more intercommunication between neurons is possible. It is not known whether this is the result of increased stimulation from the change of environment from womb to outside world, or whether the increase in synapses enables us to take advantage of that stimulation. Simultaneously the neurons increase in size, and the axons become wrapped in myelin sheaths as a result of the increased activity of the supporting glial (grey matter) cells. This process of myelination goes on for some time, the bulk of it taking place in the first two years of life. It increases the effectiveness and speed of the impulses passing down the axon, because it is an insulation, somewhat like the wrapping on an electric flex.

In other words, the developments in the brain after birth enable messages to pass more quickly, more smoothly and more widely from one part of the brain to another, and so connect up areas which were imperfectly in communication with each other before. Damage of various sorts may interfere with this development either by destroying cells or by hindering the growth of the intercommunicating systems. Fortunately the immature brain has great powers of adaptation, so that replacement of the functions of damaged areas by undamaged ones is possible. There are even cases of infants losing the whole of one cerebral hemisphere and yet developing apparently normally, because the other hemisphere was able to adapt to the disaster. This facility is largely lost in the adult, though some taking over of the function of a damaged area is possible. In neither child nor adult can the damaged area regrow like a lizard's tail. If a part of the brain is lost it stays lost.

Growth and maturation of the brain is accompanied by growing up of the child. The milestones which a child is expected to pass have been neatly packaged so that it is possible to read how your baby should have behaved yesterday, and what he can reasonably be expected to do tomorrow, next month or in a year's time.

To explain the transition from infancy to adulthood in terms of brain function, Luria suggested a possible model. He postulated that the whole brain had three functional systems:

1 for regulating tone and awakening the cortex — midbrain activity;
2 for obtaining, processing and storing information — involving mainly the visual, sensory and auditory areas of the brain;
3 for programming, regulating and verifying mental activity — mainly the frontal part of the brain.

These systems are governed by a law of hierarchical structures so that each functioning unit consists of:

(a) a primary zone of high specificity, with many nerve cells with long axons for transmitting impulses;
(b) a secondary zone processing or preparing programmes with fewer long axon cells and many more short process ones for intercellular communication;
(c) a tertiary zone of only short process cells where participation with other areas takes place and conscious activity is organised.

In the adult the tertiary zone is dominant and controls the other two. In the child the formation of properly working secondary zones cannot happen without the integrity of the primary zone, and a properly working tertiary zone is not formed unless the other two are working on the right lines. The primary zone is dominant in the child, but by adulthood its role is reversed and the tertiary one takes over. The very young child cannot distinguish the message from the noise, but the adult looks at what he wants to see and listens to what he wants to hear.

Maturity is not solely the function of the calendar; nerve cells and milestones are not sufficient to explain the whole of a child's development. Experience is a determining factor. In any one model of brain function (and Luria's is by no means the only one) the emphasis placed on environmental as opposed to neurological content varies from one author to the next, depending on his beliefs and training.

Piaget divides the developmental process into three stages:

1 a period of sensorimotor development from birth to two years, when the child extends interest in his own body to the objects of his environment;
2 a pre-operational stage from two to seven years, when the child first builds an internal picture of the world outside himself and then follows this between seven and eleven with the development of thought processes which are stable and reasonable;
3 a stage of formal operations when logical thought becomes possible.

Some workers have laid stress on the importance of the motor competence of the child in relation to conceptual development. Others maintain that sensory integrative processes play a major part in the development of perception. Their work has laid the foundations for a whole range of remedial programmes based on the improvement of the basic skills which underpin the reading process. Such models seek to explain the underlying mechanism of development. They can serve as guide lines for the investigation of a child's performance and also for the construction of a teaching programme when things go wrong. For the field worker — that is, the parent, school teacher and doctor, who read the wise books but do not write them, deal with the child and do not have time to theorise — the models are of great value if viewed as different facets of the same diamond, sending out flashes of illumination, sometimes in seemingly contrary directions.

Damage to a child's brain may be gross or subtle. If gross and resulting in cerebral palsy or a unilateral paralysis, special adult care and special schooling will be necessary. It is not the intention to discuss such cases, but rather those whose medical condition may escape the early net of adult observation and only become apparent during the course of schooling.

Four types of case will be discussed in this chapter:

1 the epileptic, for many of these children have their first attacks while in the classroom and these attacks may be so mild as to be thought to be inattention rather than illness;
2 the minimal brain dysfunction child;
3 the child with brain damage;
4 the child affected by toxic substances.

Epilepsy

Epileptics have fits; not every child who has a fit is an epileptic. A fit is not a clear-cut disease, but is a symptom of many.

Attacks may be classified by their causes, on an anatomical basis, or by the form they take. This last is of the greatest interest to teachers who may have to spot them in an otherwise undiagnosed child and set in train the necessary medical investigations.

Five types of fit may be encountered: these are labelled *grand mal, petit mal, temporal lobe attacks, focal seizures* and *small motor seizures.*

Grand mal is the classical convulsion, often preceded by warning sensations, in which the patient turns up his eyes, loses consciousness whilst jerking about on the floor. When the fit subsides, it is followed by semiconsciousness or confusion which may last quite some time.

Petit mal is characterised by very brief losses of consciousness without any convulsions, which appear for the first time during early school years and are commoner amongst girls than boys. Each loss of consciousness lasts only a few seconds but there may be ten, twenty, or thirty a day. The child appears momentarily vacant (and indeed is so), may drop whatever she is holding, and minor repetitive movements such as twitching of the eyelids may be seen. The first sign of the onset may be a falling off of school performance, with slowing of intellectual processes, the child's educational experience being as full of holes as a Gruyere cheese.

Temporal lobe or psychomotor seizures manifest themselves as periods of altered behaviour of which the child is not aware, and during which he is not able to cope with what is going on around him. They are not often seen before the child is about ten. A lot of different things may happen. The child may be very anxious and experience abdominal discomfort or pain. There may be a sense of 'having been there before', either in time or space, or the child may hallucinate. There may be outbursts of inconsequential rage. To the onlooker, the child may seem dazed, turn pale and stand staring. This can be followed by normal but out of place 'activities' — automatic behaviour.

Focal seizures do not start by affecting the whole child but begin by producing movements which the patient cannot control in a limb or the eyes. The patient is often conscious though the localised fit may spread to involve the whole child.

Small motor seizures are losses of consciousness during which muscle power fades dramatically so that the child drops to the ground sufficiently quickly to produce injury. Many of those affected had difficult births.

The relationship of epilepsy to schooling

The consensus of opinion is that if epileptic attacks are not too frequent then intellectual impairment does not occur, but that frequent bursts of grand mal seizures may have an effect because of the damage caused to neurons and because of the interruption of schooling.

No special teaching methods are necessary for epileptic children provided that their IQ is normal, their behaviour acceptable and they have no physical handicaps. They may, however, have poor concentration, specific difficulties in learning spatial concepts and with reading or arithmetic, while the drugs necessary to control the attacks and limit the effects of the disease may also produce side effects.

The results of medication may vary from drowsiness or dopiness to over-activity and aggressive behaviour, giddiness and inco-ordination, memory problems and perhaps specific difficulties in learning.

The control of medication is the responsibility of the physician alone whose advice must be sought and who bears the responsibility of deciding what level of dosage is best in any one case.

Nigel For those of us who have not seen our child have a fit, it may be difficult to appreciate how frightening it can be, especially on the first occasion. Even after the convulsion is over, there is the worry that it may happen again, and the relief brought by the umbrella of drug treatment is immense. But because of the possible relationship of some preventative treatment to educational or behavioural problems, it may be necessary to establish whether the treatment or the disease is the more important factor responsible for a learning disability. For example, phenobarbitone used to be prescribed extensively because of its undoubted effectiveness in controlling the incidence and severity of fits, but it may make a small child aggressive. Phenytoin, a more recent form of control, is suspected of being associated with poor reading unless the dose is carefully monitored.

The impact of this Scylla and Charybdis situation in the family may be seen in the case of Nigel, who was fine until the age of one when following an injection he had a fever and a convulsion. After this he had to take phenobarbitone to control his frequent convulsions which would otherwise have been damaging. When seen at the age of 9 years 6 months he was still taking it, but had not had any fits for four years. In spite of superior intelligence, his reading proficiency was three years below that expected of his chronological age. His understandably overprotective parents had removed him from school and organised home tuition for him, three times a week for one hour. Fortunately he liked his teacher who was extremely competent and in the time at her disposal achieved much. Two more years of this three-lesson week had further narrowed the gap between age and expected reading skills and he had acquired sensible and generally successful if slow strategies for coping with unfamiliar verbal tasks. However he continued to display an awkwardness in dealing with words and ideas associated with them, especially where longer pasages of print were concerned. To the Clinic staff he seemed in need of daily tuition and stimulation by his peers. Indeed his parents proposed to send him to school full time and with this in view had taken him to the local swimming pool when other children of a similar age were present. But Nigel's aggression and attention-seeking had been so violent that the timing of the swimming sessions had to be changed. His parents, having substantially dealt with his intellectual problem, were now faced with the less tractable one of social integration.

Minimal Cerebral Dysfunction

Children who have suffered brain damage as a consequence of disease or injury may show emotional, behavioural, motor, perceptual, language and other cognitive disorders as well as the signs on which the diagnosis has been based. The relationship of the damage to these after-effects has been clearly established. There are however children who show very similar disorders but lack any definite signs indicative of brain damage.

The work of Knobloch and Pasamanick has related abnormal maternal and foetal events with disorders of behaviour and language which become apparent in later years. What they wrote is worth repeating.

> 'Some time ago we constructed the hypothesis of a continuum of reproductive causality. According to this hypothesis there is a lethal component of cerebral damage which results in foetal and neonatal deaths, and a sub-lethal component which gives rise to a series of clinical and neuropsychiatric syndromes, depending on the degree and location of the damage. We found that these abnormalities range from the more obvious disabilities such as cerebral palsy, epilepsy and mental deficiency, through learning and behavioural difficulties, such as reading difficulties, tics and behaviour disorders of childhood, probably as the result of cerebral disorganization following minimal brain damage.'

The main cause of these disturbances is thought to be a decreased supply of oxygen to the brain at a critical moment in its development. Towbin has shown that different sorts of damage may occur depending on the timing of the oxygen lack. He has pointed out that the most hazardous thing that any of us ever do is to be born.

Not all authorities accept the view that there is actual damage and prefer the term 'minimal brain dysfunction' (MBD) because they feel that damage should not be assumed from behavioural signs alone and that there must be strong supporting evidence from classical neurological examination as well. Levinson feels this is cerebellar not cerebral.

Rutter considers both terms to be too vague 'a ragbag' and recommends that a more precise diagnosis be made. He suggests that this group of disorders may be divided into at least four:

1 disorders of speech and language;
2 disorders of coordination, the 'clumsy child syndrome';
3 specific learning disorders;
4 mixed types.

The last are, in the experience of the Clinic, the most frequently encountered, though, as will become apparent, usually one element predominates. This is perhaps the moment to explain that when doctors do not know why something should be so, they tend to label it 'specific' or 'ideopathic' and that it is widely held that there is no difference between the term 'specific learning disorder' and 'specific dyslexia'. It is the view of the medical co-author of this book that dyslexia is a symptom that requires investigation and that specific dyslexia is one as well, though the underlying mechanism may not be identified.

However, ragbags have their uses, and the term minimal brain dysfunction (MBD) serves to emphasise the neurological component of a child's make-up. It is up to the clinician to identify and evaluate what may be slight changes from the normal and to temper his enthusiasm for finding things medically amiss with common sense. 'Seek and ye shall find' does not mean that what is found will necessarily be of any great value.

Reference to Luria's model gives some indication of why minor changes occurring at or around birth, when the brain cells are most vulnerable and the primary zone is dominant, should have at least a delaying effect on the development of processing capabilities. Certainly one of the principal features of the MBD child is his immaturity: at seven he tears round like his two-year-old brother, while at ten he is still showing the emotional swings of a six-year-old; there may be slowness to develop a dominant hand, slowness in learning right from left, slowness in learning to tell the time, persistence in the confusion of b and d.

The part played by his environment is vital. The MBD child is at a disadvantage if the environment is not sufficiently flexible to allow for his behaviour and difficulties. His restless, sleepless, unsatisfiable activity may take the pleasure from the achievement of his birth, and good bonding with his mother may not come off. His impact on her and the rest of the family may be as much the cause of some of his later problems as is the alteration in his brain function. His needs may not be met by a school system geared to children whose neurology is intact, or nearly so. The outlook for the MBD child depends to a great extent on his family and school environment's ability to adapt to his needs.

As a counterpoise to the importance of the world around him is the possibility of a genetic element. The frequency with which the sons of late readers read late, or poor spellers spell poorly, or behave in ways which remind their grannies of their fathers at the same age, tempts anyone working in the field to believe that it could be all due to an inherited characteristic. But it is not easy to sort out what is inborn and what is due to family environment.

To prove that one or other aspect of MBD is 'in the blood', four items of evidence are needed:

1 the disorder should occur in particular ethnic groups more often than it does in the population as a whole;
2 identical twins should have a higher incidence than non-identical ones;

3 accurate identification of the disorder in near relatives must be proven;

4 siblings brought up in different environments must be investigated to rule out the possibility that up-bringing is what really matters and not the genes.

As things are at the moment, the case for a genetic factor being present is suspected but not yet confirmed.

Though MBD is a term covering a multitude of clinical pictures, only two case histories will be given by way of illustration. It is worthwhile, however, noting any biological or medical element in the histories of those cases described in later chapters and realising that this aspect will have influenced the development of the child's scholastic abilities as well as affected the course of action proposed by the Clinic team.

Nicholas After a normal pregnancy Nicholas's arrival was eventful. Weighing under 5lbs though born on time, he was blue and jaundiced, his condition being so poor that he had to be specially nursed for two weeks. After that, his development seemed normal. His milestones were passed on time, he was a stable toddler and got on well at infants' school, enjoying it enormously as he was a sociable boy who appeared to be succeeding well. However, after seven his school began to be worried about his reading and writing, and his headmistress felt that he was under-achieving. At the age of 8 years 9 months he was getting on well with his siblings, making models, building adventure camps in the garden and the local woods, singing and playing the piano. Despite having no strategies for dealing with unfamiliar words (his phonics were elementary and he made no use of context in monitoring and correcting his performance), his reading and spelling were in step with his chronological age. What then was the worry? His IQ was revealing, the verbal component being in the very superior range (WISC Verbal 144) and the performance component in the bright normal bracket (WISC Performance 114). This wide discrepancy between the two elements is well outside the normal and is indicative of organic brain changes at some stage in his life. Interestingly, his difficulties with the performance tests were not directly perceptual but rather problems with the interpretation of pictures in a sensible fashion. His electro-encephalogram showed an asymmetry of the maturation component more marked on the right side. On clinical examination there were no clear signs of permanent brain damage.

He fits into Rutter's ragbag of minimal brain dysfunction, and provides a good example of what may be encountered initially. From the doctor's point of view there is no remedy.

Neil Neil's mother was not very well towards the end of her pregnancy as she suffered from anaemia and that form of high blood pressure known as 'toxaemia'. However her delivery was normal and the infant passed his developmental milestones on time, except that as he got older he became a bit unhandy. When he went to school he was integrated and happy, but quite soon it became apparent that he was consistently behind the rest of the class, in reading but not in maths. He was given remedial help and was still having it twice a week when seen in the Clinic at the age of ten. His mother remarked that he still had difficulty managing a knife and fork and that he was no good at cricket. When examined, no abnormal physical signs were found by the doctor, though the eurythmist noted that he had difficulty in balancing and was slow to imitate her movements. In spite of an IQ in the bright normal range (WISC 118) he had a reading comprehension age of 8 years 5 months and a spelling age of 6 years 10 months. His short-term memory was poor. His electro-encephalogram showed marked immaturity for his age.

The therapy and remedial teacher's recommendations for such a case belong to the next chapter. What is important is the good example he shows of one type of MBD (or specific reading retardation, or specific dyslexia if you prefer it) in which the untoward event occurring around birth is associated with a learning disability much later in life.

Brain damage

Neville It is not only a blow to the head which will injure the brain. Infection may be just as potent a cause of trouble, but as with all cases of insult to the central nervous system, the later in childhood it happens, the more obvious the connection between the event and the effect may be.

Neville was born normally after his mother had had a perfectly normal pregnancy. He was fine until he was five, when he developed encephalitis (an infection of the brain) which made him comatose. On return to school after his convalescence he learnt to read and spell with great speed, whilst his language skills developed to such an extent that French was his favourite and best subject. However, his manipulative skills deteriorated so that, whatever his intentions, his hands would not do what he wanted them to. He was a painfully slow writer, quite unable to do justice to his intelligence on paper. He was always late in taking notes or copying from the blackboard, writing essays and compositions. Like Nicholas, there was a gap between the Verbal IQ (WISC 131) and the Performance one (WISC 93) indicative of brain damage. On clinical examination he had definite signs of damage to the neurons in his motor cortex easily demonstrable by the doctor's routine tests.

When compared to Nicholas he shows a very similar picture in his IQ pattern. His problems were limited to the performance side, but he had a story which easily connected the cause (encephalitis) with the result (poor manipulative skills, or dyspraxia) and signs of the damage were still demonstrable.

The outward similarity of a case of MBD to that of brain damage is obvious.

Adventure play-time (effect of toxic substances)

A little bit of what you fancy does not always do you good.

Turkish delight comes in several flavours. The peppermint version, if shaken up with hot water, makes a green and sticky drink which smells and looks like an exciting liqueur, but does not merit the tag '52⁰ proof'. However, if drunk in sufficient quantity and with sufficient imagination, it induces nausea sufficient to persuade an ardent twelve-year-old that he is tight. The demonstration of such a bold spirit of enquiry, such an exploration of sensory territory, will receive if not exactly applause from pedagogue and parent, at least benign amusement. When the appetite for adventure results in a largish chunk being riven from forbidden fruit, the evil apple is snatched away to cries of adult horror, the louder because it was adult carelessness that left it within reach.

An eight-year-old, who regularly injected himself with the discarded syringes from an addicts' clinic and soon became a junkie, was a rarity. His problems with reading were unimportant.

Children who experiment with lesser evils are common enough. It is important to remember that they may be in the class room, under the noses of teachers and doctors, their learning difficulties masquerading in inocuous disguise.

Norman Norman was a nice lad of twelve who had nothing much the matter with him until he fell off the back of a bus. A few months later when seen at the Clinic his memory was poor and his reading and spelling were found to be about two years behind the expected levels. The psychologist noted that he was slow and apathetic, devoid of initiative. He was said to be very aggressive at home, cringing and withdrawn in school. It was all put down to his accident until the psychiatrist, who was investigating his behaviour patterns, persuaded him to give up sniffing lighter fuel and he promptly improved all round.

We never did find out whether this was why in the first instance he fell off the bus.

Another toxin

Useful things may be dangerous. Lead is of particular interest in this respect, for it has served many useful purposes: as waterpipes, as an additive to paint or petrol, as an ingredient in articles in common use where it is locked up chemically or physically and is no risk except to those making them. As dust or fume it may enter the body through the mouth or lungs and sometimes through the skin. It may be in the general atmosphere as a waste product or in the home atmosphere having been carried there on a worker's clothes. The risk of the latter happening will be reduced by the Health and Safety Commission's new Code of Practice. If absorbed in sufficient quantities, lead may poison a child, causing acute brain or nerve damage and anaemia. There is evidence that the effects of the long term absorption of very small quantities may be poor behaviour and learning difficulties. Many studies into the degree of this hazard are being carried out currently. The extent to which lead should be incriminated as one of the causes of poor reading or spelling must wait on the outcome of this research.

Conclusion

The diagnosis and treatment of a neurological condition which may affect schooling is a doctor's job, but he needs a lot of help. The teacher may well be in a position to recognise the onset of a nervous disease, or a change in the state of a child's neurology, long before anyone else; she sees the child outside the familiar undemanding home environment, struggling to perform at the same rate as his peers.

However jaundiced a view is held of the various taxonomic cloaks that the medical profession wraps around its ignorance, teachers do well to bear in mind the neurological aspect of their pupils' performance so that they may never be accused, as Freud was by Bertrand Russell, of forgetting the brain. Throughout the rest of this book, mention will be made of biological events in a child's life which may have had an effect on his or her schooling either immediately or at a later date; they are there for the non-medical reader to notice in passing and perhaps to persuade readers to turn back to the appropriate section in this chapter.

3
Coordination and Orientation

As noted, mild disturbances in the brain may occur as a result of untoward events such as temporary shortage of oxygen at or around birth. These can result in subtle rather than gross neurological impairment and delays in acquiring motor skills with cerebellar and cerebral signs.

A typical case would be of a mother, after a difficult labour, producing a baby blue and undersized. The odds are that the baby, grown into a school-age infant, may well be slightly clumsy and not do too well at bookwork. If, in addition, infant and family live under stress in cramped housing, and both parents go out to work so that mother has no time to talk and play with her child, that child may well be language retarded and unhandy, and the scholastic demands of primary school will prove progressively less manageable. The delays in developing good coordination, efficient motor skills, definite dominance of one or other side of the body and orientation in space have varying effects which can be measured and compared with the performance expected for a particular age. The examination is time-consuming and requires special training if an accurate level of maturation is to be established. However, just seeing what the child can do gives a very good idea of the state of development. There are varying degrees of incoordination. At worst there is the child who is famous for his accident potential. He is clumsy from the time he gets upright, and leaves a trail of broken crockery and spilt liquids behind and around him. Less obvious is the fit, out-door child, who is hopeless at small ball games like cricket or table tennis, but is covered in swimming badges and comes first in the cross country run. In the same category are those with appalling handwriting and bizarre penholds.

Many of the children with reading retardation show some confusion of dominance: that is, the preferred hand may not be on the same side as the preferred eye or foot. In others, ambidexterity may persist late into childhood. This, however, is not a cause of learning disability, but another symptom of underlying neurological or developmental impairment. Firm establishment of laterality (or dominance) is not associated with a concomitant improvement in reading or spelling, unless the mechanism underlying the learning disability has also improved.

Another symptom associated with reading retardation is poor body image: the child has a poor internal representation of how the parts of himself are organised, how they function in relation to each other, and as an organic whole. This disjointed self image is always coupled with a poor ability to orientate oneself in space and cope with local geography. Because the physical self is the central point of reference for the personal environment, a confusion in its realisation will spill over into a confusion with the environment.

Weakness in coordination, body image and orientation may be improved by therapy, in the same way as the environment and its inhabitants can substantially affect the degree and rate of development of the child. Both provide stimulation, the therapy being the more intensive and specific of the two. But it is important to realise that some children are born dyspraxic: that is, they have difficulty processing and ordering incoming information. This shows up as an inefficiency in carrying out unfamiliar motor tasks; turning an unfamiliar task into a familiar one by practice may improve the performance of that task, but the underlying inability to cope with a new task remains.

There are a number of programmes for use at different age levels which are on the whole successful. Painstaking individual (or group) eurythmy, physiotherapy, ballet or movement, with or without music, will be effective. Physiotherapists, for instance, favour exercises with hoops and balls which emphasise the joint action of eye and hand. Occupational therapists take this into the field of fine movement and some develop techniques for improving handwriting. But though the motor skills improve, there will be no corresponding magical improvement in reading. Arguably this still represents a valid achievement, especially valuable for children with learning difficulties who often have few pluses to their credit. Simple contact with a jolly and articulate therapist will improve language usage, so that an advance in scholastic skills may seem to be associated with better coordination. However, let's face it, there is no firm evidence that such programmes make any difference to learning difficulties. There is no substitute for teaching if you want to learn something, and if the subject taught is arithmetic, this will not improve a knowledge of history. Similarly, if the subject taught is country dancing, this will not improve spelling.

Denis An observant infant teacher in the reception class first noticed that Denis, one of the largest children of the intake, was unusually clumsy and not particularly active physically. Four terms later his teachers and his mother and Denis were keenly aware of his total lack of progress with reading and writing, his settled reluctance to take part in playground games and the meagreness of his expressive speech. He came to the Clinic on his sixth birthday, a ponderous solemn boy, who would start speaking staccato and then tail off into a deep monotone growl rather like the sound made by the biggest teddy bears.

His previous history yielded few clues: his mother had had toxaemia at the end of pregnancy and he had had a certain amount of ear trouble; the latter could have accounted for a slight difficulty with auditory discrimination. But his receptive vocabulary was very good for his age and his understanding of verbal instructions precise. On the other hand his balance was poor and all his movements slow and incoordinated (he could not ride a tricycle); he was quite unable to copy gross movements, even after several demonstrations and being himself placed in the correct starting position. Bi-manual tasks, such as screwing bolts into nuts, were painfully slow, and the effort overflowed into other parts of the body, so that he wriggled, twisted and stuck his tongue out with the movement of the nut. Finer tasks, such as drawing a line across a page, were performed in the opposite direction to that required, and he held the pencil in the palm of his hand, like Lady Macbeth with the dagger.

Eurythmy and occupational therapy were immediately on offer, and for three months he had once weekly sessions which included exercises with bean bags and balls, hopping, pigeon walking, lying on the floor and walking various geometric shapes, numbers and finally letters. Towards the end he drew the same shapes as large as he could on a board, and last of all scaled down on paper. At the start of the school year he joined a once weekly reading group with physio-, speech and occupational therapists in attendance. The exercises continued and his efficiency in running, walking and jumping improved, ball bouncing, catching and throwing soon became reliable with the biggest ball and this was then scaled down. He ceased to have doubts about up/down, backwards/forwards, although left and right remained troublesome longer. He learnt to hold his pencil correctly, write from left to right, and his handwriting, although slow, was at the end of another four terms beautiful, showing no rotations. Also he no longer lost his way on board games. After some practice his auditory discrimination had become excellent; his voice, particularly at moments of pleasure — and he turned out to be a cheerful boy with a liking for practical jokes — rose and fell with the expected intonations. He climbed the garden toys and fought the other boys with complete self-assurance. And he learnt to read — and spell. At the age of 7 years 5 months his comprehension of what he read was ahead of the standard expected for his age, his spelling and reading accuracy commensurate with it. In view of an IQ in the bright normal range this was an underachievement, but since he never practised reading at home and his school operated exclusively on one 'look and say' scheme, his proficiency may be judged a success.

Incidentally his arithmetic, mental and written, was faultless.

Handwriting

The causes of poor handwriting, like the causes of poor reading, are many. They may be divided into three main groups, though it must be remembered that one or more causes may be present in any one case.

1 Difficulty in making the hands do what the brain commands, even though the picture of what is intended is clear in the mind, may be due to neurological disease. More simply, it may result from a lack of teaching or insufficient practice in the art.

2 If there is faulty visual perception of the shapes required, then there will be faulty production of those shapes, however intact the rest of the nervous and muscular systems between brain and ball point. Uncertainty how to spell encourages bad handwriting as a form of camouflage and is indicative of native wit rather than of disease.

3 Psychiatric or emotional disturbance may make the physical effort of writing too great for any accomplishment, whilst tension can be reflected in tight handgrip and tiny writing.

Diagnosis of the cause of poor handwriting is in part the function of the medical profession, though it may seem illogical to employ a doctor to improve poor calligraphy in view of the profession's reputation in that field. However, in the Clinic's experience, poor penmanship has been found to be of considerable importance, though it is difficult to define. At one time samples of handwriting were sent to a panel of judges, made up of teachers and therapists, but in only one case did they all agree on the quality, whilst frequently the judgments varied markedly. There is no standardised test to apply, and it is well to remember that what one person regards as bad, illegible writing, another may find quite satisfactory. In practice, unsatisfactory handwriting boils down to being either too slow, or too illegible for comfort, or both.

For school children this often means that they cannot copy from a blackboard or a book as fast as teacher wants. The obvious aid of a finger of the non-writing hand to isolate the successively wanted words from the rest of the printed page (that is, as an adventitious aid to figure ground discrimination) is seldom used. The other common accelerator, correctly formed cursive writing practised until kinetic melody is acquired, is subject to school policy. Some schools insist on fountain pens at all times; some will not introduce 'joined-up' writing before the last year of junior school; some do not give handwriting high priority so that little time is devoted to teaching and practising it. Some children though forming and joining their letters and spacing their words correctly do so with such pressure, and so much uncalled for underlining, that their rate of progress is quite inadequate for keeping up with the work of the class.

On the other hand some children, despite vagaries of letter formation (the commonest is writing the second stroke first for the letters a, y, g and d, and a completely circular o made either clockwise or widdershins) manage to write rapidly enough for junior school by using print. But with increased speed, or demand for increased output in secondary schools, legibility suffers. While the angle of individual letters seldom varies, other essentials suffer; the proportion of the letters and parts of letters relative to each other (for example, the ascender in h or the descender in y) is incorrect; letters are uncertainly formed (typically the a, g, o and d are left open, to resemble the u, the y or the cl); the strokes across t and capital A are omitted (for capitals and lower case are mixed randomly); letters are placed unevenly on the line, giving a caterpillar effect; the spaces between letters and words are irregular, and connecting strokes are covered by the next letter. An overall wobble in letter formation is rare and evokes less teacher displeasure than inadequately differentiated letters or, with older children, sudden shifts between phrases in upright cursive and cursive sloping to the right or left. Some children deliberately cultivate very small writing; older ones may have developed highly idiosyncratic ways of forming letters which add up to an illegible but highly distinctive visual pattern, which they are reluctant to modify.

The overall impression is that if teachers complain they complain emphatically. Generally they do so with good reason: unserviceable handwriting is one of the first stumbling blocks to obtaining employment. Application forms have to be filled in by hand.

David David's mother had a very long and very difficult labour. When tiny David could lie only on his left side, when a toddler he was clumsy and late in learning to dress himself, buttons and shoe laces proving almost insuperable challenges. Learning to swim was very difficult for him and his performance on a bicycle was so alarming that at 11½ his family felt it was necessary to go with him. To say that he wobbled would be understating the case; he was lavish in his use of the road, on both sides of the line running down the middle. Board games were enjoyed, but model making was out. David's handwriting, which his school insisted should be with a fountain pen at all times, was the cause of much complaint. However, his teachers were broad-minded about his spelling, though somewhat less so about his dominance of all class discussions and insistence on fanning the most trifling verbal exchanges into full scale speeches. By all accounts he was, and always had been, a loner.

David came to the Clinic at the age of 11 years 8 months, a boy with very thin legs and protruding ears, quite unable to sit still. He spoke volubly, at either shout or whisper level, and resisted signals to steer the conversation into fresh channels. However, he responded with good will and many comments to a straight request for a change of activity. On examination he could not manage activities requiring the use of both hands at once, especially if the activity was symmetrical, and he sang throughout this particular test. His gross tongue movements were slow and incoordinated, and a request to speed them up generated a lot of associated movement in hands and body. Any voluntary action was accompanied by involuntary overflow movements in other limbs. He could tell his right from his left only by looking at his wrist watch. His cursive handwriting showed no rotations and was correctly formed, but ill-defined, because the relative sizes of letters and parts of letters were very irregular, with the joins of the o, a, g, d, c and w being particularly unsteady.

The occupational therapist made the following suggestions: there should be mirror image work of both upper limbs, so that simultaneously they perform the same action. These should then be repeated sitting opposite the therapist, copying her movements. As movements on the gross scale improve, action patterns should be made smaller, for work on finer aspects of co-ordination. For direct handwriting practice, large patterns should be drawn on a wall or blackboard for David to trace over, and he should be encouraged to draw them in the air using the whole arm. He should progress to the same exercises using formal letters. These can be drawn on his back, for him to say what they are before he draws them on the board. He can also trace letters on a sandpaper board or with string shapes, and finally practise writing between guide lines, abandoning the fountain pen in favour of a Pentel. Constructional activities with clay or papier mâché should be undertaken and later upgraded to models requiring finer precision.

Speech therapy was also suggested, to link with a phonic approach to spelling, and handwriting practice of particular phonic patterns.

As he lived in the country a long way from the Clinic, the local hospital was appealed to and responded excellently. Four months after referral the Occupational Therapy Unit had developed his constructional activities to the stage of making and seating a stool, as a sustained project to link the twice weekly domiciliary sessions, and to produce rapidly a positive recognisable result.

David was seen again fifteen months after his first visit. He was much calmer in his movements, was better coordinated and was no longer aggressive or over-active. He had joined a youth club and was keen on orienteering. His spelling had shown the most improvement since his last visit, then his silent reading comprehension, whilst his handwriting was much more legible 'when I am in the mood'. It was obvious that the efforts of the local Occupational Therapy Unit had improved his motor skills, whilst his school and parents had been responsible for his improvement in mood and social performance. His spelling was admittedly well below his chronological age, in spite of his normal silent reading comprehension, but limited resources lead to careful selection of those areas where they should be spent and there are worse things than a failure to turn out all one's pupils as competent orthographists, so his teachers were to be congratulated on their achievement.

Handwriting difficulties of multi-factorial origin

Donald Donald, first seen at the Clinic aged 11 years 9 months, had many problems, but uppermost in his mind was his poor handwriting. His reading was normal for his age, and his spelling was poor; he talked too much, to the annoyance of his teachers, was pretty good at sums but hopeless at geometry, both in constructing shapes and understanding them. His great difficulty was in physically getting things down on paper, and his school had given him remedial help with this for two years, but without success.

By the time he came everyone (that is Donald, his parents and his teachers) was very anxious about the situation. Examinations showed that he had a Verbal IQ in the superior range and his Performance IQ, which has an important visual perceptual content, was at the other end, borderline normal. Unsurprisingly he had problems in this area, especially with figure ground and with constancy of shape. In addition he had a lot of physical signs of delayed motor development, had difficulty holding his pencil and was markedly incoordinated in all gross and fine movements.

This item from his range of difficulties was so severe that it was suggested that he should be allowed, and taught how to use, a typewriter for all written work. School concurred, and set about looking for one. In the meantime Donald received active therapy and drug treatment for his anxiety, to which he responded favourably. About three months after his first call at the Clinic an occupational therapist with an interest in handwriting was located within easy distance of Donald's school. He was persuaded to attend a one-to-one therapy session one afternoon a week.

A year later he returned to the Clinic, with a note from his school saying that his handwriting was now so rapid and legible that the search for the typewriter would be discontinued. He gave a convincing demonstration of his new skill and carried on a balanced conversation about *Lord of the Rings,* which he had just read.

What caused his improvement? A firm believer in the primacy of environmental factors could blame the adults for making him anxious; the neurologically inclined might emphasise the delay in maturation of his nervous system; those uncharitably inclined towards school teachers might think that nobody had taught him how to form his letters. Which chicken came before which egg? The matter is of more than academic interest.

Fortunately Donald can now write.

Topographical agnosia

Topographical agnosia is a high-sounding phrase for getting lost outside one's own front door and having difficulty with maps, both in understanding them and drawing even simple ones. It is commoner in girls than in boys, and whatever other problems may accompany it, it is unlikely that the sufferer would do well in geography, or be much use as the map reader for the driver of a car.

It is recognised and labelled 'topographical agnosia' only in older children, the ones who have encountered map reading either at school or in leisure activities such as Scouts, orienteering, or Duke of Edinburgh award schemes. It includes only tangentially the inability to remember and interpret the symbols on Ordnance Survey maps. It is mainly a matter of faulty concepts of, or direction in, actual space, as in a park, or in symbolic space, as on a map. The latter represents a further degree of complication since it involves interpreting a two dimensional medium which represents three dimensional objects.

A sense of direction is based on a reliable mechanism for orientating oneself in space. The old chestnut applies: 'How do I get to Hyde Park?' 'It depends where you're starting from.' This starting point is the concept the child has of his own position in space, and this in turn depends on the child's concept of his own body. For correct functioning he must have fully assimilated the idea that his body consists of two symmetrical halves, and have experienced this through vigorous movement in space. From movement the concepts of direction emerge:

up/down (made more concrete by gravity)

forwards/backwards (the discomfort of turning one's head to look over the shoulder is a help)

Later this concept develops into the concept of *in front/behind* and *foreground/background*

left/right (the most abstract of the three and more difficult when expressed as *east/west*)

A concept of direction involves not only moving oneself from A to B (that is oneself in relation to static objects), but also the relationship of objects to each other and the moving self, and the relationship of details within an object, as in: 'The box of chocolates is open straight in front of me. Is the peppermint cream to the left or to the right of the hazelnut cluster?' This last aspect develops into an awareness of spatial relationships between map features.

Judging all these entails the use of vision. However, the body's initial awareness of space comes through the proprioceptors, the sense organs in muscles and tendons with which position in space is first perceived. Both are needed for the child to develop an accurate consciousness of environment, in which distance, position and direction acquire meaning in relation to the position and posture of the body.

It is much easier to orientate oneself reliably in real space. 'I go down the steps, forwards to the gate, through it, turn towards the pillar box and across the road to the sweet shop.' Fortunately there is never more than one pillar box in sight, and sufferers are adept at selecting unique landmarks to act as mnemonics. By substituting concrete details for 'left/right' most children manage adequately in familiar space, because movement is related to defined tasks and situations. The difficulty lies in getting 'left/right' sorted out even with the useful phrase, peculiar to English, 'the right *hand* side', and the pun 'you write with the right hand' (which is useless if the sufferer is left-handed). Sometimes semi-permanent external aids are suggested, such as a ring or fixed identity bracelet. But the child continues to have difficulty in explaining how he went to the sweet shop, and even more how he got back—that is, telling the route in reverse. He may neither know nor understand the words for spatial concepts in general. And even if he does, he may not use them effectively to conceptualise the whole of a particular space and its component details, both in relation to each other and the space overall.

When it comes to maps, even those of a known district, familiar landmarks are disguised by symbols, the convention that north is at the top of the page is often forgotten, and there is the tempting possibility of turning the atlas round. For older children there is also a six figure grid reference. All these are additional complications of the abstract task of orientating oneself in symbolic space. In the classroom, first aid consists of not turning the atlas round, and using a tiny plastic figure who holds something pointing unmistakeably forward. Moving this toy across the map reproduces the movement of the vertical body over horizontal space, and by imagining himself inside the tiny figure and verbalising his reactions the pupil can realize the positions of the symbolic landmarks on the miniature landscape. For map reading further relevant considerations are: can he hold in mind the particular symbol he is looking for while actually engaged in looking for it? How rapidly and systematically does he search for the symbol? Can he pick the particular symbol out of the whole welter of symbols on the map? (This exercise is similar to the familiar Frostig figure ground discrimination test.) Having located it, can the pupil translate the symbol into a three dimensional image of the feature represented? This last involves a stable system of reference (one object to one symbol) analagous to the sound-symbol association required for reading, and should be acquired by the age of nine to ten years.

However, these exercises do not solve the difficulty of drawing maps of one's own surroundings. Some children start from themselves and work outwards, and very rapidly lose the shape of the whole they are trying to portray. They can draw, but while drawing they cannot hold in mind the structure, let alone the proportions, of the overall shape understood as one whole. More sophisticated children start with a moderately accurate overall shape and then cannot include within it all they perceive on the ground. Others manage the shape and the inclusions, but have 'a lot of space left over'. These are weaknesses of proportion, and may well be due to inadequate observation. After all, how many primary school children have compared the length of their beds to the breadth of the bedroom window, measured with a tape or outstretched arms and accurately verbalised their observations? In a primary school class this can be overcome by 'talking through' a map before drawing it to achieve awareness of the real features behind the map. It is desirable to draw on a large scale, and to include pictorial elevations of features rising above ground level, but only after each step has been discussed. Clearly the map drawing process is analogous to writing compositions/stories/essays. In both processes a whole has to be held in mind, and the components that make up the whole have to be brought to the forefront of consciousness in the appropriate order. Both processes are language mediated, but the visual component of map making is very much greater.

Teachers are wise to plan map-making in easy steps. There are a very few commercially available pre-map work books, but they tend to move in steps of uneven magnitude and therefore need supplementary exercises. Some have been devised by the Clinic staff, and these begin with an accurate understanding and use of words and expressions for positions in space. Better fun, and more beneficial, is joining the Cub Scouts or Brownie Guides. In a group outing to a particular spot a variety of literal points of view will emerge. Discussion will coordinate them and then correlating them with the correctly orientated map follows without loss of face to the sufferer from topographical agnosia. After a few such exercises the expertise at map-handling will have improved dramatically. According to Clinic records, no child who has been a Cub Scout or Brownie Guide for three or more years suffers from this embarrassing disability.

Derek In contrast to the other boys described in this chapter, Derek had relatively few problems; he was of all round good intelligence, with a reading proficiency in advance of his 14 years, and adequate spelling ability. His gross motor coordination and orientation in space were seemingly good, especially on the football field. But except when on very familiar ground he got lost with embarrassing frequency and maps were of little use. This was doubly unfortunate since his group of subjects for GCE O-level and CSE included geography. Also his handwriting was spectacularly illegible: tiny, with the letters formed, according to his teachers 'every which way'. Certainly the formation varied substantially depending on the position of the letter in the word, and even so was not invariable. Consequently there were many interruptions in what should have been a steady flow.

Therapy started with making himself into letter shapes while lying on the floor. It says a great deal for the rapport established with the occupational therapist, an exceptionally pretty girl, that she got him, a tall bony adolescent with large hands and feet, to do this at the age of 14. The next step was tracing simple patterns on the board, paying particular attention to the direction of the lines and the smooth continuation in flow of patterns. Chalk held in the lateral pinch grip (that is, the normal hold that most children adopt without trouble) at first proved difficult for him, but gradually became easier. The programme followed the steps outlined in David's case, but in view of the urgency to achieve an improvement Derek additionally was given handouts to trace and to practise writing large on the back of wall paper rolls at home. His map reading improved as the handwriting programme developed.

But to raise it to the desired O-level standard, the map-making programme below was devised in response to his needs, and we are glad to be able to say that he got his O-level in geography.

Map-making programme

The following programme shows some therapy suggestions which can be taught in conjunction with the pre-atlas workbook called *Let's Make Maps* by P.C. Harris and E.O. Giffard (Collins-Longman).

Stage 1

The subject must have complete understanding of the following words for spatial orientation:

in front of, at the end, above, on top, forwards, behind, together, downwards, parallel to, on the edge, upwards, over, next, beside, last, through, inwards, by, at the back, outside, on the left, close to, up, across, below, underneath, from ... to, in the middle, half way, corner, down, past, inside, before, amongst, beneath, towards, as far as, under, on the right, in between, alongside, near.

(These words are taken from one of the *Quin Reading Games,* published by Cressrelles.)

This may be done by:

(a) asking the subject to move himself into various positions related to various objects around the room, e.g. 'Sit on top of the table.'

(b) asking him to move objects around the room in relation to the other static objects, e.g. 'Put the stool in the corner to the left of the door.'

Stage 2

Right/left discrimination and orientation must be understood.

(a) The subject should be able to tell his right hand from his left, as well as arms and legs, and a little later, eyes and ears too.
(b) He could also be asked to place a hand flat on the table and to point to the finger which is on the left side of the middle finger and so on.
(c) The teacher should draw two identical objects on paper and ask the subject to join them with a line drawn from right to left, and vice versa; then, with the objects drawn in different positions, to join them with an upward/downward line.
(d) When there are several objects drawn the instructions can become more complicated, e.g. 'Join the top of the apple to the ball on the right with a line going upwards.'
(e) The subject should be asked to do the same, using objects rather than the 2D representation on paper, e.g. 'Put the pencil to the right of the book.' 'Move the pencil so that the biro is on its left side.'

Stage 3

Pages 2 and 3 of workbook.

Stage 4

Using solid equilateral shapes, e.g. triangle, pentagon, square and same scale outlines of their sides drawn on to paper, the subject is asked to match up the object to the same shape on the paper. (This assumes that the subject has no difficulty in matching up shapes.)

Stage 5

Page 4 of workbook.

Stage 6

Pattern making and copying with Kohs' blocks and peg board.

Stage 7

Pages 5 to 7 of workbook.

Stage 8

Model houses (the ones from a game of Monopoly will do), a church, school, garage and trees are needed in order to lay out a model village as on page 8 of the workbook. Work through instructions at the *top* of page 8 of the workbook, using this model.

Stage 9

Page 8 of the workbook.

Stage 10

The subject should now construct an *identical* model village beside the original, to the same scale.
'Background' and 'foreground' should be taught.

Stage 11

Pages 9 to 11 of workbook.

Stage 12

Ask the subject to describe positions of objects in the room in relation to each other, e.g. 'The window is behind the table.' Models of the village could be substituted in place of the objects in the room mentioned above.

Stage 13

Pages 12 to 21 of the workbook.

Stage 14

Ask the subject how many chairs, windows and so on he can see around the room, and how they are placed in relation to each other.

Stage 15

Pages 22 to 27 (finishing at top section '... under the railway') of the workbook.

Stage 16

Scatter objects on the floor or table. Ask the subject to measure the distances between them and describe their relative positions including measurements.

Stage 17

Middle section of page 27 of workbook.

Stage 18

'How do I get from the classroom to the dining room?' and similar questions. The subject should give verbal directions. In case of difficulty he could walk along the route, explaining where he is going at the same time. Later he should repeat the same route from memory, and eventually try drawing the route.

Stage 19

Bottom section of page 27 to end of workbook.

Scattered in the seven books of *Reading to Some Purpose* by P. Flowerdew and R. Ridout (Oliver and Boyd) there are a number of graded exercises involving words for position in space, map-reading and map-making. These would consolidate the areas covered by the programme above. The Collins-Longman Atlas series moves into formal mapwork with two further workbooks of increasing complexity, to accompany *Atlas One* and *Atlas Two* from the same publishers.

4
The Spoken Word

We listen and read in order to understand, and we speak and write in order to be understood. Obstacles to the smooth functioning of receptive and expressive language at either level generally manifest themselves in school as poor comprehension. As interference with speech development accounts for some 60% of the cases seen in the Clinic, a quick review of the normal process, together with some indication of how things go wrong, is necessary. Since learning enables us to understand and produce speech the two must be considered jointly. Hearing means not only the detection of sounds by the ear, but also the perception of those sounds by higher centres in the brain.

At birth a child has no experience of hearing, and response to sound is reflex; if there is a loud bang, he and we jump, though in those born deaf this reflex action will be absent. Any sounds made by the infant are reflex responses to other stimuli; hunger for instance makes him cry. If the hearing system is intact and if the nervous system matures and develops normally, the reflex-induced noises change to babbling. The child discovers that moving his muscles makes sounds and he works them for his own enjoyment. By listening to himself he establishes an auditory feed-back loop which tells him of the results of his own activity. This system will blossom to keep him informed later of what he is saying, as well as to control the muscles of speech, like a thermostat monitoring input via output. Faulty hearing or faulty muscle control will interfere with the establishment of this system.

After babbling the baby will begin to imitate his mother's face and throat movements and her voice, enjoying the satisfaction of getting a maternal response and rewards for the sound production that goes with it. The mother's provision of a speech environment, coupled with love and comfort, are vital to the development of language by the infant.

All sorts of things can go wrong. The child may be more or less deaf, so that noises are not received properly by the brain because the ear is not functioning properly. The ear may function normally, but the brain either does not mature at a normal rate or is slightly damaged, so that the child is unable to take advantage of a normal sound environment, since incoming signals are not processed correctly. There may be a motor disturbance, messages being received and understood, but when a response is attempted, the production of sound is at fault and the feedback loop fails to be properly established.

The necessary stimulus and model of the loving mother may be absent, so that despite intact anatomy and physiology, the child is deprived of an adequate language environment from which to learn. A mildly deficient environment and a slightly handicapped child may combine to produce a marked language retardation later.

Learning to listen to speech and finding out how to make speech sounds result in learning the sound code of the mother tongue. To understand how the ear works helps in the recognition of some of the problems of the language retarded child. Energy produced by the act of speaking sends pressure waves through the air to vibrate the ear drum.

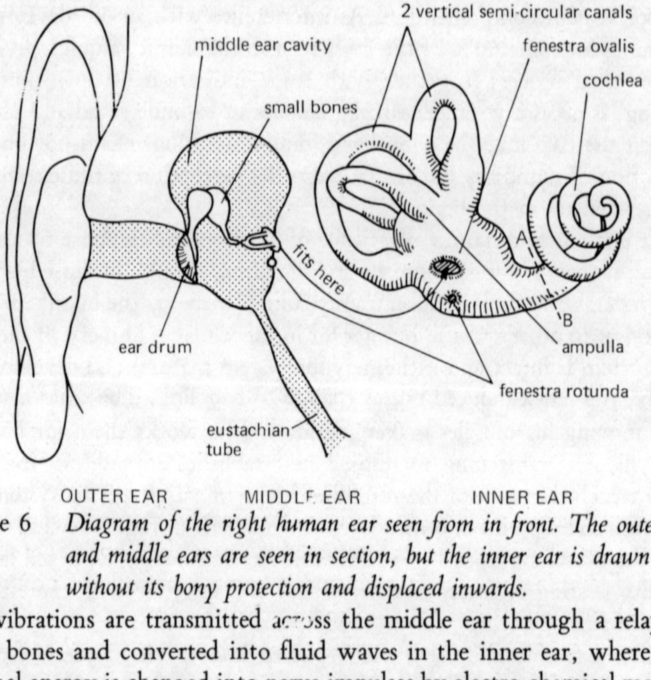

Figure 6 *Diagram of the right human ear seen from in front. The outer and middle ears are seen in section, but the inner ear is drawn without its bony protection and displaced inwards.*

The vibrations are transmitted across the middle ear through a relay of small bones and converted into fluid waves in the inner ear, where the original energy is changed into nerve impulses by electro-chemical means. The loudness or intensity of sounds is measured in decibels, which, rather confusingly, are not absolute units like inches or half pints. They express a ratio between two loudnesses, and to complicate matters they are logarithmic units. To be meaningful, the base line intensity against which the comparison is to be drawn must be known; in the same way, it is meaningless to refer to the year 1978 unless a reference point such as the birth of Christ or the foundation of Rome by Romulus is also understood. The quietest sound, that is the sound of lowest intensity which can be heard by the average human ear, is taken as the base line, or zero decibel, when dealing with human speech. The normal loudness of speech three feet from the speaker is about 60 decibels above this base line, but in general, consonants, on which we depend largely for our understanding of English, are said more softly than vowels. For instance there is just over 20 decibels difference between the initial consonant sound 'ph' in the word 'for' compared with the terminal vowel sound 'aw', when said by an Englishman. A Scot will of course confuse matters by sounding the 'r', which is quieter than the 'aw' but louder than the 'ph'. A child with a slight hearing loss could have difficulty hearing at least some parts of each word spoken by a softly-voiced teacher at the other end of the classroom, but no apparent hearing loss when addressed face to face with 'Now pay attention, Jane.'

Sounds, as well as being loud or soft, are made up of waves of different frequencies. The mechanical acts of speaking alter not only the intensity or loudness of speech sounds, but also the frequency, which is measured in cycles per second. The human ear can cope with sound waves between 125-8000 cycles per second. Pure sounds of one frequency are practically impossible to produce and most speech sounds are made up of several frequencies with two main components, one low and one high. The low frequencies give the sound noise and the high ones make it easy to differentiate from other sounds; if the low part is lost it is as though the speaker were far away, faint but audible; if the high part is missing, the speaker can be heard but is difficult to understand.

The sound code of English has 40 phonemes, (that is, 40 minimal units of speech sounds) which must be learnt in order to understand and be understood in that language. Interference with speech sound discrimination, and especially with the high frequency component of a phoneme, results in poor understanding of what is said, however loud it is shouted, or however near the teacher is to you. Fortunately there is a simple but effective test which serves to screen out children with difficulties of speech sound discrimination. Some phonemes are more difficult to pronounce than others whilst some are used more often than others, so the young child acquires first the easy ones which he hears most often: 'p' and 't' are learnt sooner than 'r' or 'th'. In any event, by the age of seven a child should have mastered all 40 phonemes and be able to recognise, articulate and choose the correct one for saying what he wants.

Along with the maturation of the nervous system, learning to listen, development of a feed-back system and increasing command of the phonemic code, comes an increase in the number of words recognised and used, though receptive vocabulary is always greater than the expressive one. A child's active vocabulary increases from 250 words at the age of two to ten times that number when he is seven. The syntactical and grammatical structure of sentences also grows from two-word phrases consisting of nouns at the age of two, to the sharing of logical ideas through the medium of seven-word sentences at seven. Language can develop normally, but vocabulary, and therefore understanding in a vocabulary rich environment, may be restricted if the home vocabulary is limited. If mum is out at work all night as a nurse, and dad is at work all day, and neither talks to the child, or if one talks one language and the other another, so that the child ends up with a smattering of both, he may be at a disadvantage when he gets to school.

To illustrate these points, six types of case will be considered:

1 The effect of a foreign language environment at home, one tongue being spoken at home and another at school or in the street.
2 The impact of intermittent or mild hearing loss on the child who has already developed speech normally, prior to the onset of the trouble.
3 Poor discrimination of speech sounds. This may be very difficult to recognise in the classroom as an entity separate from general poor comprehension, but teachers must be aware of it as the handling has to be very specific.
4 Poor comprehension of what is written in spite of an apparently good reading-out-aloud performance.
5 Poor expressive language.
6 As a subdivision of the above, poor ability to sequence sounds correctly.

Foreign language environment (mother tongue at variance with English)

It is called one's mother tongue because that is what it is: the language surrounding a child from birth plays oyster to create the pearl of speech. Come the age of five, if the language spoken at school bears no resemblance to what is spoken at home, little harm is done provided the school is informed and the child has developed normal use of his mother tongue. Even so, on starting school he will be temporarily isolated through his lack of serviceable language. It does not have to be a language of the kind taken at O-level. One small five-year-old created a problem in a South London school where the staff were well used to dealing with pupils from different language environments. Having tried him in English, French, Italian, Greek, Spanish and Gujerati, it was not until the doctor asked him where his home was, and received the reply, 'Doon the wa'er', that he was identified as the only Scot in the school.

If the adults around a child use two languages freely, and omit to make this clear to teachers, so that it seems as if the child came from a one-language environment, quite a lot of confusion can result. Greater difficulties arise if the child is attending a national school on Saturdays, or in the evenings, or in the holidays, not just to keep up the language, but also to stay in step with another educational system. Much confusion, cultural as well as linguistic, can result if no one language and set of customs have been acquired first. Linguistic development too slow for scholastic comfort in either language is a common if less drastic outcome. In later adolescence this can spill over into doubts about identity, particularly if the two backgrounds are also materially very disparate, such as council housing and ice-cream trading in Dundee during the bulk of the year and regular long summer holidays in a village south of Salerno.

There are variations on this theme. An English father may have married a non-English wife who, knowing no others, will sing nursery rhymes in her own language and play her own finger games with the child, so that his early kinaesthetic patterns of tongue, mouth and throat movement are not those that he will he required to use in school. The converse is apparent if a non-English speaking father, who hopes to return home one day, marries an English wife, speaks English of a kind at home, but sends his child to the paternal language school.

Albert Two partially developed languages do not add up to one normal one, but if they did Albert would have been in a strong position linguistically. His French father had married an English wife and Albert was the second child. Born normally, he was a voracious little baby with nothing abnormal in his motor development or medical history. The language of the home, if not the nursery, was French, and the family lived in France until Albert was five. On moving to England he started at an English infants' school, but only stayed there for a year and half before moving on to a French-language school. To make matters worse, he was taught to read French at school at the same time as he was taught to read English at home by his mother. This series of disruptions — family, school and language — landed him aged 9 years 6 months in the Clinic, where he was very difficult to assess in anything except English. Superficially he seemed to speak quite well, although when faced with a reading test of phonically grouped words he asked whether they were French or English. His vocabulary was found to be one and a half years below that expected of his age. Exactly the same situation was identified when he was tested by a French speech therapist, who found a huge lack of basic vocabulary in French, below average comprehension and immature syntax.

The only way out of this impasse is to choose one language, and stick to it, without hesitation or deviation, but with repetition, until the vocabulary and syntax, and therefore comprehension are developed to the degree required by education and family expectation.

This is the counsel of perfection, applicable in the case of Albert and the two other cases that follow because these concern families who had made a clear decision as to which country, language and culture was their undoubted first choice; also in each case the parents were capable of communicating with complete ease both in the chosen language and the original one. The problem is much less tractable, and much more common in inner cities, when one parent, especially the mother, does not know enough English to communicate with her children's teachers and peers. Furthermore she may not know, even in her own language, the words for concepts her children are being taught in school in English. In these cases a family cannot be expected to adopt wholeheartedly a language which would ruin its internal communication system, limited as it already may be by differences in education and experience between the generations. But it is necessary to remember that these children's higher academic attainments may be permanently restricted by imperfect command of the language of instruction.

Ann Ann had a devoted grandmother who did not speak English, and equally devoted parents who did. The whole family lived in an isolated farmhouse in an area where TV reception was poor. Consequently when Ann started school at five she found herself unable to compete with children who had been speaking English exclusively and vigorously all their short lives. She so failed to communicate that she was thought to be deaf, but her hearing was found to be normal. She was next thought to have suffered brain damage during a febrile convulsion at the age of one, but upon detailed examination the neurologist dismissed that theory. Her school, ignorant of the grandmother's influence, suggested that her intelligence might be well below average. When she came to the Clinic at the age of six, an attractive little girl with an intent stare at everyone in turn, she had made no progress with reading or writing. When spoken to she echoed stereotyped repetitive phrases in reply. She knew correctly the names of six colours and could count up to five. She had no idea of her age, address or 'phone number, and was unable to talk spontaneously about her home, answering specific questions about it with only yes or no. When asked to describe a picture shown to her, she enumerated the objects in it, omitting all detail. Her speech was explosive, quick and at times difficult to understand, not because there was any articulation problem but because she confused the grammars and sound systems of the two languages. Her understanding and use of English were at the 3 years 9 months level, insufficient for coping with lessons or playground activities. A delicate balance between weaning her from granny's language and destruction of a happy relationship had to be struck. Just how the parents did this we don't know, but they did, and she is now scholastically indistinguishable from her peers.

Andrew Having to cope with two languages was bad enough for Ann, but Andrew at the age of six was expected to manage three: Serbo-Croat at home and English outside the door, except on those frequent occasions when he went for a walk with his grandfather, to whom he was devoted, when Greek was the preferred language. An added refinement was that his parents came from different provinces of Yugoslavia, each spoke with the intonation characteristic of the region, and these in no way overlapped. Unsurprisingly the few words that Andrew spoke were delivered in a flat monotone like the Daleks. He was large for his age, always hungry, with torn jerseys and socks at half-mast, quite unable to remember the names for items of clothing or food. And yet all his family were multilingual; under pressure of joy, anger or plain hurry, they side-stepped nonchalantly in mid-sentence from one language to the other, never losing the thread of the argument or pausing for thought or breath. They did not appreciate that at some time each one of them had had only one language, which later formed the scaffolding on which to hang the others. Poor Andrew could not understand, read or spell much in English, which was not very surprising to anybody except his parents, who, cheered by discovering that he had a high IQ, were depressed by his inability to cope at an English-speaking school. It took two years of speech therapy and remedial help to give him a personal language in English. The remedial teacher used to feed him secretly during the Tuesday sessions. In the Thursday speech therapy sessions he was encouraged to describe what he had eaten, oral sensations forming a basis for speech. This seemingly frivolous approach worked. Ham proved a great developer of language. At the end of two years his comprehension and use of expressive language had reached the level expected for his age, if not his intelligence, but he continued to speak with a marked central European accent. His command of English regularly deteriorated in the school holidays, being at a particularly low ebb at the start of each academic year.

A common factor in these three cases was the ability of the child to communicate adequately within the family, but not on reaching school.

Two distinct strands emerge from these cases.

A child may be unable to cope in school because, despite normal language development in the language habitually used at home, his English, the language of instruction, is too undeveloped to enable him to take instruction in it. In London language centres deal very efficiently with a proportion of these children, and their subsequent scholastic progress is generally satisfactory.

A child may suffer from aberrant language development because of early linguistic confusion. This too will look in the classroom like very delayed language development, and he too will be unable to take instruction in English. But the treatment for his disorder is best initiated by a speech therapist and then pursued in conjunction with his teacher.

Speech sound discrimination

There are children who, in spite of having normal acute hearing, are not able to distinguish speech accurately. The ability to discriminate between speech sounds, especially confusable ones like 'm' and 'n' in 'sum' and 'sun' or the 'v' and 'th' in 'vow' and 'thou', develops gradually. If the pace is slower than average, understanding of what people are saying will be retarded. If the sounds which go to make up words are not accurately identified the gist of the conversation or lesson may be lost; it is like listening to a half-understood foreign language. There is also difficulty in establishing the association between the sound and the corresponding letter, so that reading and spelling suffer. Efforts to improve these last, even if conducted on a one-to-one basis, will fail unless the underlying problem is recognised and tackled first by the speech therapist, before any intrusion by normal remedial teaching.

Children with such a difficulty may appear to be deaf, but a pure tone audiogram will show that this is not the case. They prefer to play with younger children, whose development of speech sound discrimination is at the same level as their own, because of course they use and understand language of similar sound complexity. To adults they appear inattentive; efforts to hold their attention, or to clarify instruction by elaboration and embellishment, will fail, since any chance of the child understanding what is said is drowned in a flood of unidentifiable speech sounds. If the child is of normal intelligence and if the degree of handicap is slight, he will use visual abilities to compensate; he frequently develops a good vocabulary and when older has little difficulty in understanding what is written.

Mrs Austin Mrs Austin, for example, had had difficulty in learning to read at school, and by the time she left she had achieved little academically, never having passed any exam. Before getting married she worked in a shop, and by the time she was middle aged she was reading for pleasure, but knew her spelling was atrocious. Her audiogram, vocabulary and comprehension of what was said to her face to face were normal, but she found telephone conversations hard to follow, and talks or news on the radio meaningless. Her speech sound discrimination was poor. This was highlighted by her reading performance, for her comprehension of what she read aloud was at the 6½ year level, whilst her silent reading comprehension was adult. Her case illustrates the after-effects of this kind of language disorder, which, if recognised early enough, can be rectified.

Alan Alan was in this fortunate position. He was a good-looking boy in the first year of comprehensive schooling, whose lucrative hobby consisted of making up bicycles out of parts from rejected old ones. Obviously he had a lot of common sense, as well as a formally ascertained good average IQ, and his hearing ability, vocabulary and reading were normal. He was however a poor speller, and his speech sound discrimination was the significant factor in this, as he had particular difficulty with consonant differentiation. The remedial programme suggested by the speech therapist is shown at the end of this section (pages 50-1), and this was put into action by his remedial teacher. Within three months his speech sound discrimination had become normal, and only then did the job of reteaching him spelling begin.

Alexander The case of Alexander, a boy in the second year of junior school, illustrates specific discrimination problems. He was a shy boy, with superior verbal and performance intelligence, and a good vocabulary, and yet his reading ability was just below that expected for his chronological age, and his spelling was so poor that he achieved no score at all in the spelling test. Predictably, in school he hated 'spellings' and singing. His language comprehension was poor; long, grammatically complex instructions had him floundering briefly before giving up. If encouraged to try again he generally refused, and when taxed with this said his teachers at school complained about him in the same way. His auditory discrimination was so poor that he made 19 errors out of a possible 30. He had difficulty in hearing the difference between similar sounding words where only one sound was different each time. Exactly the same type of mistake was also made in a word recognition test where the stimulus is oral and the response demanded visual. To help his language comprehension the teacher was asked to keep instructions concise and clear, and to request him to repeat them back before acting on them. Exercises suggested to help this aspect of his problem are also listed at the end of this section (see pages 50-1). Most importantly he was given the usual programme for improving speech sound discrimination and when seen eight months later he had improved markedly.

This time he made only 10 mistakes. Two of these were /f-th/, /v-th/, common enough in London children. Two more were the vowel sounds in /gall-goal/, /suck-sock/, and the rest were difficulties in discriminating final voiceless plosives /-p/versus/-k/, /-t/versus/-p/, and voiced plosives /-g/versus/-d/, /-d/versus/-b/. His comprehension of what he heard was practically normal and his reading comprehension had improved by twelve months. He was spelling poorly, but at least to some extent.

At the age of transfer his auditory discrimination, language comprehension and reading skills were satisfactory, but his spelling lagged two years below that expected at his age.

Sound training: an example programme

1 To help to build up the concept of differences and similarities in sound, some training needs to be given first in identifying and comparing non-speech sounds:

e.g. listening to short samples of music and then saying whether the tunes were the same or different;

listening to notes on a piano and giving an opinion about possible similarities;

comparing and matching sounds made when rattling match boxes filled with different materials such as nails, pins, rice, or beans.

2 The pupil should be given a logical way of classifying and comparing speech sounds that does not rely on visual or auditory perception alone.

e.g. explain *where* sounds are made:

lips: p b m
tongue and teeth: th
lips and teeth: f v
tongue tip and teeth: t d n l s z
tongue and roof of mouth: sh ch zu (as in measure) j
back of tongue: k g ng

e.g. explain *how* sounds are made (with the voice or breath):

breath: p t f th s sh ch k
voice: b m n ng d l r z j g

3 The above training should lead to the auditory identification of sounds, first with the help of watching the speaker's mouth, then later with the speaker's face covered. It is important to choose sounds that are widely different.

For example:

the 'stop' sounds p t d k could be compared with 'continuant' sounds m n ng l s,

or 'voiced' sounds b g l d could be compared with breath sounds p k t.

These are only samples and do not include the full range in each group.

4 The next stage is the comparing of words that are the same accoustical-

ly except for one consonant change. Initially this should be an auditory task *only* so that there is no confusion with the visual vowel changes (note/coat).

Lists of words should be made and the pupil asked to say if they sound the same or different. The list should start with wide contrasts and lead to narrow contrasts.

For example: pin: chin
pin: tin
pin: sin
pin: fin
pin: bin
pin: pin

Initial and final changes should be introduced with emphasis on the *differences* and not the similarities.

Example words: cat: cap
arm: art
eat: eel

5 The above leads to the formation of links between the *heard* and written symbol.

At this stage the *Tutorpack* programme and machine (Packman Research, Twyford, Berks) is a good aid.

Words should at first have the same written vowel symbol.

Work on vowels should come late as these are much harder to hear and have so many different written symbols.

Hearing loss of later onset

As has been mentioned earlier, in normal speech there is a difference in noise level of about 20 decibels between vowels and consonants. If hearing loss occurs after normal language has been established, the result is not overall poor language development. The problem is one of being able to hear clearly what is said and therefore being able to understand long discourses. With a slight loss it is easy to concentrate for a short time, or if the subject matter is familiar, but attention easily flags and the listener becomes fatigued with effort. Children with mild deafness rapidly learn to use clues gleaned from a speaker's face and body movements to eke out their hearing: they also do very much better in the one-to-one situation when there is no outside distraction. There is evidence to show that such children have difficulty in mastering school tasks unless visual teaching methods are employed.

The picture which a child with mild deafness of late onset presents is well illustrated by the story of Alison.

Alison Alison was a model baby after her mother had a normal pregnancy and delivery. She walked and talked early, passing all her milestones when expected. She had several attacks of middle ear infection before she went to school, and at four and a half was found to have 'glue ears'. In this condition fluid collects behind the drums and has much the same effect as stepping on the soft pedal of the piano — noises are muffled and speech can only be heard if loud and clear. The condition is relieved by the insertion of grommets in the drums to drain the glue out so that hearing may improve.

By the time she was eight, her teachers were bothered as she was not making progress in spite of an IQ in the average range (WISC 109). A diagnosis of dyslexia was made by an educational psychologist. It is right to say that a child is dyslexic, in the same way that it is right to say that a child has a fever, provided that investigations are carried out to discover why. Anyway, Alison received remedial help on a one-to-one basis and her reading comprehension at the end of it was above that expected for her age. She still did not do well at school.

On examination at the Clinic, she was found to have normal oral language development except that her discrimination for consonants was poor, especially if she could not see the speaker's face. She had a hearing loss of 40 decibels in her right ear (a mild degree of deafness) whilst the hearing in her left ear was normal. Matters were made worse for her as, being a good biddable child, she sat at the far end of the classroom with her back to the teacher, in such a position that to turn her good ear towards the latter she had to twist round over 180°. She relied on the friend who shared her desk for information as to what was going on, because she knew that she did not always understand what was said.

When seen by the remedial teacher at the Clinic, she was a nice-looking little girl who moved quickly and gracefully. She settled to what she evidently expected to be a tiresome session with hands clasped in her lap. However, as the interview progressed she relaxed and explained, with an increasing peppering of giggles, that she was terribly slow at getting things done, especially when it came to writing stories when she couldn't think of 'the sort of words teachers like'. She also felt at a disadvantage over spelling, as she never had more than two-thirds right in the twice-weekly word test, and in maths problems when 'It's very hard to find out which sum to do.' As she went on to talk about her friends in and out of school (her social life was very active), her hobbies (she was a tennis champion) and her family, her smile became wider and her gestures more exuberant.

Tests showed her to read aloud slowly and inaccurately, but still retain a good grasp of the subject matter. The inaccuracy was due to ignoring punctuation (and of course omitting all expression) and substituting for the printed word others that bore little visual or auditory resemblance to the printed one (although generally the ends of the words tallied) and made little sense in the context. A further test showed that she had very uncertain methods of tackling words that included a number of clearly defined phonic patterns. Her handwriting was neat, well formed and quite rapid when she knew how to spell the word, but with little idea of phonic break-down of unfamiliar words her spelling was her weakest area by far.

Since her receptive vocabulary was also below average for her chronological age it was suggested that her vocabulary should be formally expanded on a phonic basis by exercises from John Smith's *Spelling* Books 0 - 9 (Cassell), and the Ridout and Holt workbooks *Words 1-4* from their *All Round English* series (Longman). Her mother was asked to read to her daily from longer and more difficult books chosen by Alison so that the active use of the expanded vocabulary should be encouraged. Corrective reading aloud was unlikely to be a long-term chore; it was suggested that the start should again be on a phonic basis, to encourage the habit of careful examination of words.

In short, it looked as if the recommendations were partly directed towards a change of work style, necessary to come up to standard in her academically inclined school. Alison's and her mother's out-going cheerful temperaments accepted this suggestion, particularly since it was allied with a request to change Alison's seat in class, so that she would always be able to see the teacher's face. The school agreed, and at the time of writing she is, as far as school goes, living happily ever after.

Poor comprehension of speech

Classroom observation will reveal the child who fails to understand being spoken to in his native language. The teacher's and other children's vocabulary may be obviously unfamiliar to him; the sentences addressed to him too long or too intricate; the teacher's language may suit senior classes but be above his young, linguistically undeveloped head. When teaching a small group the teacher can easily identify the uncomprehending youngster: he will have lost interest, stopped listening and often started disrupting the class. But he is much harder to pinpoint, especially if he is well behaved and smiling, in a class full of busy comprehending children. While his comprehension may be uncomfortably below average for class work, it may be adequate socially, particularly if he is accepted in the playground by younger children who are operating at a language level equivalent to his own.

In any one child poor comprehension is a symptom resulting from perhaps more than one cause. Specialists will tend to emphasise the importance of the findings which relate to their own disciplines. But generalists, in this case parents and teachers, do better to remember that while specialist opinions are enlightening, the whole child and his domestic context have to be considered.

The environment may not be sufficiently rich in language of any kind; alternatively, whatever language is used as the currency of thought at home may be different from the English used in school.

A child may be mildly deaf, or more commonly intermittently deaf. In consequence he may fail to acquire speech sound discrimination at an early age, or he may fail to catch the drift of home conversation unless specifically spoken to.

Anxiety arising from emotional disturbances either at home or at school may interfere with attention or the ability to learn.

There may be a mild neurological deficit which results in psychological disturbance, identifiable by the speech therapist as a poor sound sequencing ability, or a specific memory defect.

The diagnosis of such complex factors is the speech therapist's job; equally she must dictate any decision with regard to therapy. But the teacher should be aware that such problems can exist and that they will affect comprehension and therefore learning. Even in those cases where the language of the classroom is just within the compass of the child and superficially there is no problem, poor language development may become apparent when understanding of what is read is investigated. If a child is not much good at knowing what is said, the odds are that he will not be much good at understanding the finer points of what is written.

Andrea Of Andrea it could truly be said that her problems were deep-rooted: both her parents had difficulties with reading and spelling; when pregnant, her mother had an eventful time with a severe bout of 'flu and a rise in blood pressure. The birth was stormy: Andrea was a breech presentation, slow in starting to breathe, and had to be fed by tube for a week. However, all milestones were passed normally, except that she did not speak until she was three. She received no speech therapy, went to play school at four and to infant school at five. Although she had lots of friends at school and at home, was cheerful and helpful about the house, the teacher was worried because 'nothing went in'.

She came to the Clinic at the age of 6 years 6 months, a chatty and co-operative little girl who used for single words a vocabulary normal for her age. But she was in trouble with longer utterances: her understanding of verbal commands was very poor, with a tendency to perseverate, that is repeat words, and to reverse and simplify commands. When answering questions she would start speaking, let the sentence trail off, and then after a slight pause with a fresh surge of energy, latch on to her last spoken word and build a phrase on it, often contradicting what she had said first. She could neither read nor write, not even her name; although she could, after being started off correctly, count up to ten, she could not answer the question, 'How many sweets have you got?', even if she held the sweets in her hand. At the hospital she received speech therapy to improve her ability to 'listen' and comprehend what she heard. For school it was suggested that she should be given very simple classifying activities like sorting out beads by colour, books by the picture on the cover, or distributing one pencil to each child, or two straws to go with each carton of milk. Any activities involving simple counting and vocabulary extension into simple phrases were recommended, with the *Oxford Junior Workbooks* mentioned as a framework for written comprehension. More classifying activities could go on at home, perhaps sorting out the vegetables into separate containers; a running commentary for activities such as laying the table or helping to make a cake were also suggested.

Despite not receiving any remedial teaching (apart from implementation of the above programme), two years later her composite linguistic age was only two months below her chronological age. Her auditory memory, which had been weak, remained so and she retained, although to a lesser degree, her difficulty in coping with long complex instructions. On the other hand her reading comprehension was within normal limits even if her spelling was still atrocious. The speech therapist went to the school to explain the nature of Andrea's difficulties and the necessity for presenting information to her in small chunks rather than large, and to her, indigestible ones. For children such as Andrea over-elaboration only serves to confuse. In these cases making all instructions and explanations simpler becomes the teacher's much more difficult but unavoidable chore.

Arthur Arthur's dad was totally illiterate, but his mother made up for this, and had always worked to support the family as well as bringing up her two children. Arthur walked early, but did not talk using sentences until he was 3 years 6 months. When he first went to school he was thought to be deaf, a common reaction to children with poor comprehension of the spoken word. The matter was investigated, but when nothing abnormal was found, it was dropped. Arthur was brought to the hospital at the age of seven because of temper tantrums and bed wetting, and referred to the Clinic by the Child Psychiatric Department as he could neither read nor write. He had a very short attention span, and great difficulty in understanding what was said to him; he answered all questions with 'Yeah.' In due course he was transferred to a small boarding school in the country, where he enjoyed woodwork and flying kites, but unfortunately no speech therapy came his way despite recommendations that he needed oral language development before all else.

Four years later he returned to the Clinic, this time quite chatty, especially about skate boarding, which was the craze of the period. However, his expressive language continued to reflect a marked poverty of vocabulary, and he had definite problems understanding what was said to him, especially if a grasp of prepositions was required. Again his problem was explained to his teachers and they were warned that he would not understand long or complex instructions. And again it was suggested that any extra help should be directed towards oral comprehension rather than bother about his continued total inability to read.

He returned at the age of thirteen. This time he answered all questions adequately and started a spontaneous conversation about his chopper bicycle. His comprehension of the spoken word had improved dramatically as a result of remedial help directed at oral comprehension. His reading test results also showed great improvement on earlier performance. From no reading at all, he now had a reading age of 7½. If you don't think this is an achievement, remember that on his first and second visits he had not understood what was said to him. Now he was no longer like a foreigner in his own country.

Although the child who is underachieving in relation to his own age group is the more obvious problem, there is also the child who underachieves in relation to his intelligence. His problem is perhaps more personal than social, and of greater importance to himself, his parents and teachers than to a statistician preparing reports on reading achievement in a particular district.

Anthony When seen at 8 years 6 months Anthony was nervous and uneasy and, though he was able to concentrate well, tended to get carried away by his own talking. In conversation he did not seem to grasp fully the essence of what was required or asked, and he easily became confused. On formal assessment he made errors of comprehension and in this respect was not up to the standard of his verbal expression. His IQ was in the very superior range, both in the verbal and the performance elements, but his reading comprehension was only just above the mean for his age. All the staff of the Clinic were agreed that his academic performance was not a true reflection of his intellectual ability. This had been the view of his school, who had referred him for assessment as he had difficulty in concentrating and could not spell or express himself adequately on paper. He had been having remedial help. This was redirected to include mainly comprehension exercises with special emphasis on vocabulary extension and cloze exercises; analysis of maths problems that involved several steps performed in logical sequence; any out-of-school activity to encourage close attention to detail and particular sequences, such as card games of patience, two board games ('Trafalgar' and 'The Business Game'), and model-making. Finally his family, who were very willing to help, were asked to ensure that without fail he read aloud for fifteen minutes daily from a book, chosen with the help of the local librarian, of sufficient length and complexity to engage his attention in depth and increase his command of the language of books.

Fourteen months later he had improved a lot all round. He understood verbal instructions and was able to perform sequential tasks correctly; in general conversation there were no crossed lines and he appeared to monitor his contribution closely. All the literacy skills scores had risen by more than elapsed time, and were now well ahead of his chronological age, consonant with his IQ. Three remedial lessons a week and the controlled parental contribution had worked wonders for the self-confidence as well as the academic performance of this co-operative lad.

Because so little is known of how the brain really works, it is not surprising to meet children who seem to have no clear reason for their problems. The ill-remembered partial views of adults are poor materials from which to make an accurate diagnosis, but often the few crumbs of possibly significant information are enough to make each specialist fulfil Bernard Shaw's assertion that no man can be a pure specialist without being, in the strict sense, an idiot. In the case of Adam both the physician and the psychologist felt that there were reasons in their special fields of knowledge which accounted for his truly very grave lack of understanding of what was said to him, but really both were turning the goose of an idea into an insubstantial swan.

Adam Adam's mother had married twice: by her first husband she had a daughter who continued to live with her and made life a misery for Adam, her son by her second husband (who though able to read well as an adult had had problems at school). The pregnancy and delivery were normal; Adam weighed 7lbs at birth. From the first he was a grizzly, wakeful baby, who however made good progress and passed his milestones apparently normally; perhaps he had been a bit late making sentences, his mother could not remember the time, but she had not been concerned about his speech development. He had two bouts of unexplained high fever when tiny, and pneumonia when aged two. At infant school he was said not to concentrate and to be overactive and restless. His work was felt to be below standard, and he received extra individual reading lessons at school, starting when he was 6 years 6 months. Finding that these made no difference, the school felt that there might be something radically wrong with him, and so he came to the Clinic at the age of eight.

His mother said that he was a very obedient, loving boy, with friends both in and out of school. He enjoyed playing card and board games, but would not sit to paint or draw.

He was polite and friendly, answering questions with one word answers. He said he enjoyed singing, Cubs, judo and having his father read to him. Conversation was slightly disjointed, for some questions were met with a smile, a glazed look and then either silence or a word that did not relate to the question. At other times he just changed the subject. On specific testing for auditory comprehension by the speech therapist he was able to repeat instructions verbatim (he was found to have a good auditory memory), but was not able to translate them into actions. His score on this test was exceptionally poor, and the therapist considered that he had a definite problem in understanding what was said to him.

She considered that at this stage of his language development no amount of reading tuition would help him. Her suggestions, to be implemented in school and at home, relate to an earlier stage of language development and are quoted verbatim.

> Adam needs help from a speech therapist, in co-operation with his teachers and parents. All should be aware of his marked difficulty, since it has such obvious implications for all types of learning.
>
> All instructions and questions put to him must be very short and clear. Structured work is to begin at a very basic level.
>
> 1(a) The teacher should point to things or persons around the room and name them.
>
> (b) Adam should then do the same.
>
> (c) The parts of his body and then the parts of the teacher's body should similarly be identified.
>
> (All these exercises should start with one thing at a time then two, three, etc.)
>
> 2 Adam should carry out movements on command, first whilst the teacher is doing them as she gives the instructions, and then repeating the movement by himself. This could be made more complicated, the teacher gradually phasing out her movements.
>
> 3 The teacher should have various objects, or pictures of objects, which are big/small, red/green, etc. Ask Adam to show the big ball, the red flower, etc. — next, the little blue ball, the big yellow flower, etc., gradually increasing the complexity of the commands.

4 The teacher should ask him questions, within his ability, requiring a 'yes' or 'no'; some of them can be straight forward, others can be 'non-sense' ones. It must all be fun and done without pressure or emphasis on failure.

5 The teacher should read a brief passage to him and ask a question on the contents. It is possible to go through a whole story like that, then to read the story again and ask him to tell it back.

Poor expressive speech

Adrian Adrian was an only child, born by Caesarian section; in spite of being overdue he weighed under 7lbs. His early years were said to be uneventful, and he was not noticed to be a late talker. When he first went to school at five he hated it, screaming and crying every time he was taken. Needless to say, he did not do well, but had settled down by the time he was referred to the Clinic at the age of nine, although his school, parents and family doctor (who referred him) were concerned that he could read only a few words, and could not say the alphabet or the months. He was said to be good at maths and to have lots of friends. In all this time he had had no special help.

On examination he was found to have difficulty following rapid instructions and in formulating descriptive sentences, but had no difficulty when cued in by a question, so that he appeared to need a model sentence structure to imitate in his own speech. His lips, tongue and palate appeared normal in size and shape, but his tongue movements were slow, and he could not hold a lip position for more than a few seconds. There was a slight weakness of his soft palate and of the left side of his face, so that movements were freer on the right and he seemed a little lopsided. His left hand was clumsier than would be expected in a right-handed child. Articulation of most speech sounds was normal, though three phonemes, or sounds, were consistently mispronounced, nor could he imitate them. His comprehension of vocabulary was that of an eleven-year-old, yet his oral reading comprehension was at the 6 years 8 months level; when reading aloud his miscues were either refusals or wild guesses. He was a non-speller, and wrote lower case print, with many letter rotations.

He was given remedial teaching twice a week: in cursive handwriting, to reduce the incidence of rotation and give him a visible record of progress, and in phonics, to provide a strategy for tackling unfamiliar words when reading passages of continuous prose. When reviewed nine months later his problem was more obviously one of expressive speech difficulty with abnormal articulation, and his reading comprehension was unaltered. He was therefore given a short intensive course of speech therapy to correct this, and continued with his remedial lessons. He worked extremely hard with the speech therapist and after two months of co-operative effort had made such progress that he was discharged. When re-examined a further nine months later his reading comprehension had improved by seventeen months, and he seemed a new boy.

It is important not to think that all the credit can be claimed by the speech therapist, for the part played by the remedial teacher was in this case crucial, whilst his mother and class teacher were also called in to reinforce her work.

Angela Angela's mother had labour pains during the sixth month of her pregnancy, but did not lose the child. At term the delivery was eventually normal, but Angela became jaundiced after two days, and remained so for a week. Her mother suffered from depressive disease for some time, and while ill had difficulty in communicating.

Nothing abnormal was observed until Angela went to infant school, when she was thought to be generally backward, and had difficulty in learning to read and write. At nine she was given remedial help for one term. She was a happy child, very good at sports, with a keen competitive spirit on the games field.

When she attended the Clinic at 11 years 3 months she was found to be of average intelligence, but to have a vocabulary comprehension at the very bottom of the normal population scale. Her understanding of spoken commands was adequate but slightly immature, and she had a poor short-term memory for what she heard, made worse by mood, poor concentration, or fatigue. Her upper jaw was asymmetrical, her upper teeth sloped to the left, but her articulation was normal. The speech therapist considered that her poor vocabulary was her main problem in expressing herself adequately. Her reading and spelling were about two years behind the expected level.

With this sizeable backlog of basic skills to make up, it was suggested that from the end of the academic year French, which she found confusing, should be discontinued; also piano lessons and practice, a time-consuming daily task, should be dropped at once. This would leave time for language work, partly on the basis of formal vocabulary exercises from an English course complementary to the one used in her school. Reading for fun was also strongly recommended, and a list of books geared to teenagers' interests and graded for reading difficulty was supplied, with the suggestion that she should talk about the contents in an effort to ensure she had understood what she had read.

A year later her school and home programme had not altered and she still had great difficulty in expressing herself, especially when describing places or situations. When asked to describe an object she used an adequate but very basic sentence construction. She was under considerable pressure at school and very far from happy. Her reading and spelling remained approximately two years below the level expected at her age.

Positive help to improve her vocabulary was again recommended, with two further additions: that she should listen to Radio 4, especially short stories and serials, because it was quite obvious that she had no time or inclination to read for fun; secondly, any 'free writing' that was required of her should be done orally, dictated into a tape recorder, in order to get her expressive language moving without the intermediary chore of getting her thoughts on paper in comprehensible form. Her mother was gloomy about the prospects of the school accepting the latter suggestion — and she was unfortunately, right.

Sequencing sounds

The inability to recognise the correct order of small units of speech, that is, the inability to process correctly the sequence of sounds, presents as somewhat comic talk, and if it persists into school years, overflows into writing.

Angus Angus' mother was not well during the pregnancy and towards the end suffered a rise in blood pressure (not that this is by any means always associated with the picture Angus in due course presented). At birth he weighed 8lbs and was a remarkably good baby; he did not cry 'for months'. He walked when he was just over a year old, but did not talk until he was three, and then in a jargon that was barely intelligible. He was asthmatic and on one occasion had pneumonia.

It was not until he had been at school for a year that he finally reached the speech therapists. When seen at the Clinic at the age of 9 years 7 months, a cheerful tousled boy with a wide smile, it was because of a very specific difficulty in writing accurately to dictation.

Investigation showed that his IQ was average, his comprehension of what was said to him, his auditory memory and speech sound discrimination all normal. He understood what he read silently considerably better than when he read out aloud, in silent reading his achievement age was 10 years 2 months, being particularly good on syntactical connections, and in reading aloud 8 years 5 months. On a formal test his spelling was found to be only a little short of the standard expected at his age, but significantly his spelling mistakes were the same as his miscues in reading aloud: syllables and letters were omitted or transposed. When reading aloud he tackled words several times before a version that satisfied him emerged. This involved a considerable effort, during which the gist of the story tended to get lost. Yet his performance on all scholastic tests was not seriously below par and would not by itself have caused worry. But he had great difficulty in saying his surname and when speaking confused the sequence of sounds, especially 'm' and 'n'. This was unfortunate because he lived near Wimbledon Common, which he pronounced 'Windlebomb Conom'. The sequencing problem was reflected in the test of repetition of three sounds in correct sequence, when he made a tremendous effort but was completely unsuccessful in saying rapidly the sounds of the letters 'b', 'd' and 'g'.

Since his handwriting was poor it was suggested that handwriting practice based on phonically grouped words taken from vocabulary exercises such as the *Blackwell's Spelling Workshop, or Spelling* 1-9 by John Smith (Cassell) might be helpful, on the principle that visual spatial sequencing — with which he had no difficulty — should be brought in to strengthen his memory for the structure of words. His grasp of syntax was reckoned good enough to provide the additional monitoring needed for writing complete sentences and longer passages. A final suggestion made to his mother for informal help at home was that the local junior library should be approached for taped stories which he could listen to while following the text closely.

We don't know what happened, but he is a good clinical example of this type of difficulty.

Readers may wonder why this chapter has no description of a child who has difficulty with auditory organisation as defined by Bradley. In the authors' experience the inability to 'group together words which are different but which have sounds in common' is part of a larger difficulty with speech sound discrimination which has to be corrected first. But obviously practice with categorising sounds would have been the next step in the case of Alan (page 49). In the case of Barnaby (pages 100-1), who was older than Alan, some difficulty with categorisation seems to have persisted. Both boys came to the Clinic long before the publication of findings and later remediation programme. Their problems were remedied by speech therapists in the normal course of action.

5
Speech and Written Language

The previous chapter dealt with difficulties resulting from some shortcoming in oral language, either receptive or expressive. In many cases it is perceived primarily as poor comprehension of the spoken word, but the reasons for the poor comprehension are numerous — it takes a speech therapist to tease them out, and they vary with the age of the child.

Young children have underdeveloped short-term memories, have not fully mastered the rules of the language game, and have little ability to process language logically. Older children are slow to understand complex instructions and to extract information from longer passages, slow to turn ideas into speech and have poor word-finding ability. They use semantic substitutions both when speaking and writing. Typically, in the classroom they make particularly heavy weather of any request to 're-tell in your own words'. And it is harder if the re-telling has to be in written form.

Even at its simplest, written language is not just oral language plus a large and complicated visual component. The symbols, auditory and visual (for the proficient reader/writer they are fully interchangeable), making up the words are loaded with meaning. Assuming that there is no trouble in perceiving the visual symbols (such difficulties are dealt with in Chapter 6) and that the vagaries of English sound-symbol association have been mastered, comprehension, the extraction of meaning, may still fail to take place. Alternatively the ideas may be present but it is impossible to get them on to paper in comprehensible form. In the first instance the child can manage the small units, phonemes, morphemes and words, in both the visual and auditory channel, but cannot grasp the larger units of meaning. In the second case the large units are present—or at least averred to be—in the mind, but are not transformed into the small units which will add up to a meaningful mosaic. In both cases the child cannot hold in mind the multi-layered process and bring forward in appropriate order all the layers which make up the whole. In both cases, the controlling element is the semantic content of language, which includes the whole weight of the child's language development and knowledge of life.

The differences in the degree of oral language development which children bring to reading in themselves influence the understanding of written language. The plight of children for whom English, the language of reading and instruction, is a foreign and imperfectly understood one has already been described. Similar is the case of children who, for one reason or another, have exceptionally poor vocabularies. (At the time of writing the author is teaching an English eleven-year-old who six months ago did not know the meaning of 'puppy', 'lawn' and 'zoo'. Granted he has never been to a zoo, and is always packed off to bed, television-less, at 6.30 p.m., but teaching him requires a different approach from that needed for a little Sri Lankan whose family is hell-bent on 'doing the sights'.) These children may say 'arm' when they mean 'finger', and are just as likely to write 'see' when they mean 'look'. In extreme cases the writing of a composition is impossible, but in an effort to please a young child will produce pages of imitation writing, squiggles, loops and lines in groups, which from a distance look like words, but contain only a few recognisable letters and have no meaning. Such children have no problems with copying, so beware the one who sits next to 'my friend'.

Reading progress will start faltering at a later stage for the child whose oracy is adequate for family and peers at play, but restricted not so much in vocabulary as in sentence construction and finer shades of meaning as expressed by grammatical forms. For these children oral communication, with variations of tone and facial signals, presents no problems, although their utterances are fragmented, only the most basic constructions are used (the subordinate clause even if introduced by the demotic 'what' is totally absent), and differentiations of tense and singular/plural ignored. None of this matters in face-to-face communication, it is part of the charm and humorous affability meted out by these children to their teachers. But it will militate against their comprehension of Sir's posh language and, more seriously, of the mildly formal transactional language used in many text books; producing more than half a page of comprehensible written work and anything more complex than a list will go against the grain. As adults they may know enough to understand the instructions on a packet of DIY equipment, or to fill in a form applying for a driving licence. But in their case the written language of more serious newspapers and books is not the adjunct and substitute of well-developed oral language, only a very partially deciphered map to vaguely perceived territory. Here, quite possibly, be dragons, lurking in the sequence of:

> failure to read above the level expected of a nine-year-old, leading to progressively more serious delays in language development, leading to less precise and more superficial comprehension (as well as missing out on the information and experience at second hand to be obtained from books).

Another possible obstacle to the efficient use of written language is poor short term memory. Teachers are very familiar with the pupil who is well able to 'tell his story' but who by the time he has written the first sentence has forgotten the rest; he then goes through successive reinventing cycles, taking more or less notice of what has already been written. He has a poor memory for self-generated receptive speech (see page 71 in this chapter). Less common is the pupil with a poor memory for externally generated speech. Between the reading aloud of a passage and the hearing of questions about it – sometimes a period of no more than fifteen seconds — the sound of the passage has slipped its moorings in the memory, so that it cannot be internally re-sounded and scanned for the extraction of information. Alternatively as has already been mentioned, the correctly sounded words have evoked so few responses in the child's private dictionary that many of the sounds are too devoid of meaning to yield the required information. Another possibility is that the succession of correctly sounded words, each understood at the time of reading aloud, has been scrambled in the memory into such a jumble that no meaning can be extracted. The results of the speech therapist's tests have to be considered with those of the remedial teacher to suggest what kind of memory defect is implicated in the failure of comprehension.

In the whole field of language development the contribution of the speech therapist is essential, but so is co-operation between her and the class teacher. If good results are to be obtained the teacher, in daily contact with the child, will put into practice and consolidate what the speech therapist has recommended or started in individual treatment sessions. In short, poor speech development will affect all aspects of learning. It must be recognised, analysed and corrected as early as possible. Competence with written language cannot be expected if the earlier, spoken language, stage is significantly out of kilter.

Poor comprehension of what's written (tinkling cymbals and symbols)

If it were not for Humpty Dumpty's explanation, who would know what a Jabberwock looks like? The poem is easy enough to read, but Alice was not alone in finding that 'it's rather hard to understand'. With it Lewis Carroll has demonstrated that it is possible to read accurately without any real comprehension of the printed words.

Children who do this are known at the Clinic as 'tinkling cymbals'. The phrase is borrowed from St Paul's letter to the Corinthians, referring to speakers who utter the right words (expressive language tinkling) but lack the essential ingredient, in his case charity, in the Clinic case meaning. These children do not understand what they, quite correctly, read aloud. It is the symbols which tinkle to them. And it is not presumptuous to say that it is one of the characteristics of these children that they are surrounded by love and charity, their poor comprehension being due to causes other than a lack of affectionate nurture. Like poor reading and poor handwriting, poor comprehension coupled with accurate reading has many causes, but it is always associated with poor development of receptive speech.

Teachers will be most familiar with this problem in pupils for whom English is the second, and secondary, language. They are frequently adept at getting their tongue round long and complicated English words but unable to answer, orally or in writing, even the simplest comprehension questions. Unfortunately, several reading tests commonly used in schools test accuracy only; even more unfortunately, the figures for Reading Ages obtained from these tests are often used as the basis for grouping the children in what are aimed at being well-balanced teaching units. It is therefore quite possible to find such a child, a native English speaker, in the third year of comprehensive schooling placed in a fast moving set, and his teachers puzzled: 'Why isn't he coping?' If the problem is identified at this late stage, and, in the absence of intensive one-to-one remedial tuition, a move to a less demanding set is suggested, that doesn't always turn out to be the answer. Will the pupil react negatively to the move by turning to truancy and disruption? In the case of one fourteen-year-old girl the move was flatly refused, and the refusal backed by the parents, on the grounds that the new proposed set was made up of unacceptably rowdy youngsters.

However, if a tinkling cymbal is recognised sufficiently early the results of therapy are excellent. It is noteworthy that the great majority of Clinic patients in this category were, at the time of referral, either receiving additional tuition outside school or attending independent schools, and the suggestion of referral came from the teacher.

Another characteristic these children share in a Clinic setting is their lack of personal impact. Quite simply they are difficult to remember individually. They are recalled by some parental quirk ('Do you remember his mother was knitting an enormous scarf?'), or some irrelevant event ('I think she came on the day those Americans with the cine camera were visiting'). In short, while Clinic records declare such children to be unmistakeable tinkling cymbals, it takes a lot of conversation to re-visualise them vividly enough to be written about.

Anthea Anthea talked at an early age, but was catarrhal and had asthma, as well as a history of ear infections. When seen at the Clinic at the age of 9 years 5 months she was found to have a slight bilateral hearing loss, average intelligence, and while she read as accurately as a child of nearly ten, her comprehension was not as good as that of a seven-year-old. The speech therapist found her verbal comprehension and speech sound discrimination were below average.

When interviewed Anthea, freckled and with a big smile, was quite explicit that she attended school less often than her peers because she 'was ill every two weeks'. She did not like school, nor her teacher, and admitted to being very slow at writing stories. She was receiving, indeed had received since infant school, special reading tuition two or three times a week provided by three separate teachers. In class she was helped by 'my friend', with whom in her spare time she went swimming or to a club.

While reading a story aloud, she frequently sought clues in the illustrations and when these proved unhelpful she tackled unfamiliar words by guesswork, the first letter of her version corresponding to the first letter of the printed word. She made no use of her limited but reliable skills in phonic analysis and synthesis which another test had revealed her to possess. Her guesses fitted neither the story line nor the grammatical framework and she made no attempts at self-correction. It was obvious that frequent and structured remedial tuition would have to continue, consisting of oral and written comprehension exercises of every kind. The commonly-used series *Reading to Some Purpose* by P.Flowerdew and R. Ridout (Oliver and Boyd), available in her school, would need supplementing with oral exercises from tapes, with cloze exercises and with games and drama activities to encourage both expressive and receptive speech. And of course regular attendance would be an advantage.

Unfortunately the school did not go along with this. She continued to have 'help' from three different teachers, and a year later the situation was unchanged.

Alistair Alistair, a boy of bright normal intelligence, had always been a catarrhal child and as a result had over a long period suffered some degree of hearing loss. Happy and humorous, with lots of friends, he had never been a success at school, despite great efforts by his teacher and parents to improve his reading when he was about six. Unfortunately the reading tuition placed great emphasis on the ability to read mechanically, so that when he first came to the Clinic at the age of 10 years 10 months the speech therapist found that he had considerable difficulty in understanding passages of text, but little trouble with single words. In tackling stories aloud he read with startling rapidity, complete accuracy and very limited comprehension; in terms of reading ages his rate of reading was well beyond any figures given as test norms, his accuracy was equivalent to 12 years 8 months, and his comprehension 9 years 5 months. Even when asked to read slowly he did so only — and marginally at that — when reading a war story which, he volunteered, he thought interesting. It was therefore suggested that abbreviated versions of the standard war books, perhaps *The Wooden Horse* by Eric Williams, or sci-fi such as *The Prince in Waiting* by John Christopher, should be read for homework, with comprehension questions to be answered in writing, while in school formal comprehension exercises relating to whole passages would be emphasised. Listening to the radio news and discussing it informally at home was seen as a possible parental contribution.

Alistair returned to the Clinic at the age of 12 years 10 months. By then he had followed his brother to a secondary school with an academic reputation and had been placed in the bottom stream. The discrepancy between his accuracy and comprehension of reading had slightly narrowed, with the result that he now always recognised and recalled the main idea of a passage. If allowed to re-read the passage he was also able to locate explicitly stated single items of information. But even with repeated re-readings recognition of cause and effect relationships was haphazard and inference quite beyond him. He admitted to difficulty with most types of comprehension exercise set in school.

In these cases, the Clinic suggests that one subject should be dropped, and the time so gained devoted to graded comprehension exercises. At secondary school age these should be based on the texts that comprise the curriculum and others that immediately support it. Teachers often need to prepare additional exercises to cover all aspects of comprehension, starting with literal comprehension of explicit statements. The stages are detailed in the Barrett Taxonomy 'Cognitive and affective dimensions of reading comprehension' (reprinted in *Measuring Reading Abilities,* by P.D. Pumfrey, Hodder & Stoughton, pp.131-4). Teachers in a hurry find it a useful check list, to ensure that home-grown exercises progress steadily through ascending orders of complexity and sophistication.

Children like Alistair seldom use two easy forms of self-help.

First, read and take in the title of the passage being used for the comprehension exercise or, for younger children, look at the accompanying illustration. This will bring to bear unconscious knowledge of the topic, narrow the field of possible vocabulary, and impose, however tenuously, a framework of expectation in which informed guesswork can take place.

Secondly, read the comprehension questions before reading the passage for the first time. This serves to direct attention to the desired points of information, inference, or vocabulary.

To acquire these two useful habits it may be necessary to get the pupil to talk through them several times before he commits himself to written answers.

Archie Archie was an adopted child, so nothing was known of his prenatal and birth histories. At the age of three he was uttering sounds which nobody understood, so he received speech therapy and by the time he came to the Clinic aged 9 years 11 months he spoke intelligibly, although some sounds (e.g.'sh'for's') were substituted. By this stage he was, despite bright normal intelligence, the oldest pupil in the remedial class of an academically very demanding school, with reading ages of 8 years 9 months for accuracy and 7 years 4 months for comprehension. Most significantly his verbal comprehension and auditory sequential memory were below average. He had difficulty in following syntactically complex instructions, but his hearing was normal and had always been so. He was a cheerful boy, with buck teeth, a big smile, a passion for cricket and was still undaunted by realizing that however hard he tried he could not remember what he had read, or what had been read to him. Fortunately his school was very understanding and organised twice weekly tuition in school time with a specialist remedial teacher. She visited the Clinic and a programme was worked out.

Instructions and information were to be presented in small chunks, at first only two items at a time plus a third one to follow obviously from the first two, as in: 'Pick up a red pencil, borrow a ruler and draw a margin in your English book', or, for spelling: 'The seat on the beach faces the sea'. Formal comprehension exercises were to concentrate specially on practice with reorganisation and inference. Activities involving 'learning by doing' were to be encouraged and the local Cub Scouts filled this part of the specification with excellent effect. In general he needed as much verbal contact with adults as could possibly be managed.

Tuition started at once, and the parents arranged for it to continue in the holidays. Seven months after his first visit to the Clinic his comprehension had improved to level peg with his accuracy in reading. Another seven months later all his reading skills had improved sufficiently (that is, measured higher than his chronological age) for him to be out of the remedial stream and following the school's normal curriculum, including French and Latin, keeping 'about middling' in his class. He admitted that he was kept very busy in term time and that he missed the cosy friendliness of his former one-to-one remedial sessions.

Written expressive language

> 'He's a very nice lad, open, cheerful, cooperative, good at games, good at all oral discussions, good general knowledge, grasps new ideas quickly, he reads well, his spelling's not bad, but he just cannot express himself on paper.'

A significant proportion of the children seen at the Clinic arrive with that particular label. Often they are well aware of their weakness: 'I know what I want to say, but it comes out all wrong'; occasionally they are venomous, 'I hate writing poems'; more often they are baffled, 'Miss doesn't like what I write.' Teachers and parents (and most of all parents who are also teachers) have been known to wax indignant: 'Look at this mess,' and a thirteen-year-old's essay consisting of one and a half pages of large writing is brandished, 'no paragraphs, no punctuation, words left out, a muddle and far too short.'

The youngster, on being taxed with the same essay, is emphatic that a short muddle is better than a long one. But for purposes of analysing his weaknesses and offering advice too little is of less help than too much. So an exercise book full of essays is preferred to the one-off from a loose leaf folder.

Since no formal normative test of free writing standardised on a United Kingdom population exists, the evaluation and consequent advice are subjective. But it is as well to clear the decks by first examining the handwriting: is the physical act of writing so onerous as to render all written work a punishing chore? This is seldom the case (see Chapter 3, pages 30-4). In general, small scale and clearly structured written tasks, such as sentence completion exercises, are performed easily in acceptable handwriting.

The second hurdle to clear is the spelling: has it reached the 'reasonable phonic alternative' stage, and even if not, can the writer read his text with understanding both to himself and to the class?

One area of confusion that can be mapped without too much trouble is the surprisingly common ignorance on the pupil's part as to what is meant by 'imaginative' or 'creative' writing, or 'poems'. He asks to have the specification spelt out in unmistakeable words. It is a bold teacher who offers a commentary on Aristotle, but visual aids lead to genuinely illuminating discussion. A travel brochure photograph of Venice alongside a version of the same view by Canaletto, Turner, or John Piper invariably brings out all the arguments historically advanced for and against non-figurative art. But the point is probably best made by a photograph of a pond with water-lilies next to Monet's 'Basin aux Nympheas' complete with Japanese bridge. Add the same painter's tenebrous irises from the National Gallery, and the discussion will move to symbolism and layers of meaning. This is an important step for pupils who have difficulty with inference and figurative language.

More than one lively discussion period is needed to sort out the difficulties, mainly among juniors, with sequencing units of meaning. These are children who have worked their way competently through compositions based on sequences of pictures. The early stages of these have lists of useful words added to each sequence, or if in strip cartoon form, balloons with conversation. However, once the visual prop has gone, the pupil is asked to describe something from his own experience. The topic will be chosen for its definite story line—it may well be an account of a journey. The result, after a well-judged opening sentence will often be a complete muddle. The sentences referring to particular incidents are in any old order, and some important elements in the sequence, which might have served as anchoring points, are left out. It is worth examining the spelling for mistakes of letter order and letter omission.

A lengthy but reliable remedy is to get the pupil to break up his 'essay' into sentences and write each on a separate slip of paper. At this stage his first spontaneous corrections will occur. Next ask him to put the sentence slips in the order in which events happened. Then settle down with him to discuss the order in which he has placed the sentences, reading each slip in turn and correcting the spelling and grammar as necessary. When the order has been decided, read the whole through to him to pick out any remaining mistakes of order (since a real journey is being recalled there should be less scope for muddle) and make sure that no statements contradict each other. For instance, if a suitcase has started by being blue and ends up brown, has it been dropped in the mud, charred, or has there been an interesting case-switching incident? These questions are partly designed to keep the discussion lighthearted, so that the pupil doesn't feel embarrassed by admitting that he simply forgot. When all the sentences follow one another in the appropriate order, get him to copy them out neatly. Finally, analyse the finished story into a brief plan with numbered points, each summarised ideally with one word only. Next lesson give the title for the composition, again relating to something from his own experience, and ask him to start with the plan. Discuss the plan and clarify it if necessary. Ask him to write the composition, with each numbered point on a separate piece of paper. Then continue like the first time.

Clearly this is a time-consuming way of coping with the problem and not one that lends itself to class teaching. But in a one-to-one or small group set-up, four unhurried sessions as described above are sufficient for the pupil to master the planning of simple essay writing, so that the larger units of meaning fall into the appropriate place in the sequence.

With older pupils a frequent complaint is that the given subject is dealt with logically but very superficially and far too little is written overall. If pressed, the pupil declares that he doesn't know what more to write or how to expand his thoughts. Enquiries are made what, if anything, the pupil reads for fun, and the list given in reply is generally limited to comics, magazines connected with a hobby which can be anything from electronics to collecting comics, and in exceptional cases the sports pages of a tabloid. This linguistic diet needs enriching with some literature, so a list of short fiction books, graded for readability, is handed over. The suggestion is made that stories on Radio 4 could profitably be background noise while bikes are mended or models made, and that regular listening to 'A Book at Bedtime' might be used as a negotiating point in arguments about going to bed.

For direct help in class, teachers can start with exercises designed to extend sentences, but these are mainly found in English books designed for junior school pupils. With complete essays the following tactics have been found useful. Take a piece of paper and make wide margins on both sides. With a pen of one colour and writing on alternate lines only, write an essay of the habitual length. Read through, count and note the number of words. Now take a pen of a different colour and expand the sentences written. Read through, alter as necessary, count and note the number of words. Take a pen of a third colour and repeat the process. Finally make a neat copy.

Granted this process also requires close attention by the teacher and is successfully accomplished in a one-to-one or small group set-up. But again it does work, and after several attempts the pupil can manage creditably on his own. Obviously the growth of the reading and listening habit has an excellent longer term effect, because it supplies models of vocabulary and phrasing. Much more resistant to remediation is the pupil who presents all the above difficulties. He shows no aptitude for the multilayered sequential process where the whole (the overall plan) has to be kept firmly in mind while the parts (the individual incidents, or arguments or impressions and their connections, the words to express them, the grammar, spelling, handwriting and punctuation) are brought into play in turn at the appropriate stage in the sequence of composition.

Shock treatment is part of first aid: hand out the title, allow five minutes for thought and notes, and let him record his essay on a three minute loop tape. Play it back. At the end of three minutes he will either be in full spate or, much more likely, having charged at the topic with enthusiasm he will after half-time rapidly fizzle out. Play the tape back a second time, but piecemeal, discussing with him the relevance to the title of every phrase, and its place in the sequence of ideas. By the time this is finished he will be ready to start planning his written work.

Again he needs a sheet of paper, divided unequally into a beginning, a middle and an end. Then jointly, consider the title. Perhaps 'Crumbling Cliffs' (one subject in the 1979 ILEA junior school leavers' composition paper). Does he see it as a disaster movie or a poetic description of geological processes? This will set the tone, and ideally the pace, of his essay. Where is he watching from? Is he an omniscient observer, telescoping time, a mountaineer with the ground crumbling under him, or a sailor watching it all from a vessel some way out? Considerations like these will determine his first sentence. Make a note in the section marked 'Beginning'. Next, consider the end. Will the storyteller fade into the blue, be crushed by rocks, drowned in the sea, rescued by friends or strangers? Make a note of the decision, for it will affect the middle. Now think about the physical movement involved, with gestures to help summon the most telling words, and write a few in the appropriate sections. Repeat the processes for sounds, appearances, sensations, feelings. Can he visualise the whole sequence of events like a film on colour TV? Is the story to be told in the first person? How many sections does it fall into? This will determine the number of paragraphs.

Reload the recorder with a clear tape and get the pupil to talk into it for three minutes using the words from his plan. Play it back. Then play back the first attempt, and compare the two. If the second attempt is satisfactory he can dictate it to himself from the tape, so that in committing it to paper he has only punctuation and spelling to worry about.

Arguably the above is a jejeune way of approaching free writing, and certainly there are infinite variations in the planning and construction of essays. But the pupil who cannot manage free writing coherently has to be given a few very obvious and simple crutches that he can use on his own, for everyday purposes, without aspiring to become a Hardy or a Stan Barstow.

Three books are immediately helpful:

Express Yourself Correctly by S. Kanelli, (obtainable only from Zeno Booksellers, Denmark Street, London WC1);

Advanced English Composition by S. Kanelli (Evans);

From Paragraph to Essay by M.L. Imhoof and H. Hudson (Longman).

And what about the adolescent who can't think what to write? Aristotle, simplified, will help. Just about every school subject will lend itself to consideration under four headings:

1 What is the idea behind this?
2 What are the physical means needed to achieve it?
3 What actions or processes have to be gone through to achieve it?
4 What is the end result?

Elaborate as necessary. The essay will still fall into logically connected sections.

Apparent failure

Older school children attending the Clinic for the first time fall into two main groups: those with good oral language development and those without. The articulate, comprehending school leavers get jobs however badly they may spell or express themselves on paper. They may not get the job their parents hoped they would, but nevertheless they earn their living and are successful once they know what they want to do. The inarticulate, poorly comprehending non-reading school leaver is faced with a much greater problem. These latter adolescents add up to some 8% to 10% of the children seen annually at the Clinic. They have all been through normal schooling, some may have had remedial help and, being co-operative and friendly, they come at their parents' instigation. Parents have good reason to be worried, for in the hard world outside school one of the first hurdles that an applicant for a job meets is the employer's questionnaire, a form to be filled in on the spot, asking for details of education, past employment and often of illnesses. Inability to read it will easily be spotted and the employer may well choose a candidate who can complete it in preference to one who cannot. Few firms have spotted that reading ability is in no way connected with good workmanship, no more than reading ability and entrepreneurial success, as Somerset Maugham well knew.

However scientifically determined, remedial teaching for the non-reading fourteen or fifteen year-old may do no more than raise the almost non-existent Reading Age a year or two, to a still useless level. 'Well done, Jimmy, you are reading much better' may be true, but what matters is not the 'gain' but the use to which it can be put. The purpose of investigations carried out by the Clinic for these older non-readers is different from that for the younger child. For the child it is important to find out what is wrong in the hope that it may be corrected; for the adolescent the bus has already been missed, and what must be identified are the strengths rather than the weaknesses. A real difficulty is parental over-expectation; the dreamy nimbus of hope and ill-defined ambition that surrounds the new born has not entirely faded. A long conversation, sometimes more than one, has to take place to encourage parents to see their children in new roles which are both satisfying to the individual and socially acceptable. The difficulty lies in shifting the parents' view of the problem from the black or white, 'Let's cut our losses' or 'With another push it will come right', to a previously unconsidered grey area, 'He can manage this, he likes doing it, it's a valid contribution to the community, let him get on with it.' Clinic success in this area is variable.

More acceptable is the Clinic's immediate practical response: a list of basic literacy skills (such as addressing an envelope and knowing the months of the year in correct sequence) which teachers in schools cover under the guise of 'community studies', '...the sort of thing,' as a remedial teacher nearing retirement said, 'that I made sure my sons knew before they did their National Service.' But since that day the ability to read the notice in Police Stations stating the rights of the arrested is included in the list (see pages 77-80), which also mentions several books and teaching programmes of immediate use. Beyond this, endless battering away at the first two Rs is counterproductive.

What is needed is training in a trade, so that there is something to offer on leaving school. Any skill taught must be one that the student wants to learn, be within his competence and have relevance to the local employment situation. It is important to teach him what will give him a job (and he often knows what job he would like to do). This is, of course, understood by the educational authorities in schools, as witnessed by the various sixth form courses, which include work experience and are linked to courses in Colleges of Further Education. These run excellent foundation courses (a euphemism for teaching something useful to the non-reader and managing a bit of language training on the side) and precisely targeted vocational courses. Recent examples of these, developed within the ILEA, are the Basic Clerical and Vocational Preparation (Clerical) courses. Work experience is compulsory with the latter.

The scope for expansion is considerable. But clearly no single school or College of Further Education can provide training for the whole gamut of marketable job skills: capstan lathe operator, forklift truck driver, blacksmith, bicycle repairer, hairdresser, commercial cook (not Cordon Bleu), plumber's mate, scaffolding erector, to name a few. The essential is that training should be available as a matter of course and, equally it should be a matter of course for the remedial teacher to follow, sit in on the skill training sessions, find out precisely what is being taught, and after consultation with the skill experts, develop literacy and numeracy teaching materials bearing directly on the skill taught. The whole spectrum of DARTs ('directed activities related to text': Lunzer and Gardner, 1979) can be built up. Granted that subject teachers who are timetabled, often at short notice, to teach the non-achieving fourth and fifth year pupil have to discover a new versatility in their own professional skills, with the help of books such as Mary Hoffman's *Reading, Writing and Relevance* (Hodder and Stoughton). Extra work is always involved. But the non-reader who is lucky enough to get on a DART-backed skill course stands a good chance of earning a living and perhaps even learning to read as part of the trade training.

Auriel Auriel weighed 3 lbs at birth, and the spoon in her mouth was silver if not antique. She received the most expensive of educations and was brought to the Clinic at the age of 15 years 8 months, just prior to her GCE O-levels. She went through the tests at a gallop and her reading comprehension, both silent and oral, was that of an eight-year-old. Her understanding of speech was normal, but when asked to describe school work she had difficulty in stumbling through a few phrases using a very limited vocabulary. In contrast, when speaking about her animals, she was accurate, detailed and entirely fluent. She was a friendly, biddable and slightly grubby child, markedly gauche, colliding with the furniture and then giggling in embarrassment. Her nails were bitten (but 30% of children's are), her hands slightly shaky, and she was scared in case she was found to be 'loony'. Her intelligence was average. Her headmistress considered her difficulties sufficient to hinder the reading and understanding of examination papers, quite correctly, since Auriel was expected to take, among others, O-levels in history, English literature and Greek literature in translation. The background literature course at her school included *The Idiot* by Dostoevsky. Reasonably enough she coped better with the fishes, tortoises, birds, gerbils, hamsters and dog that she kept at home. She wanted to learn animal management and knew where she wanted to go for job training. No such luck. Her family had other ideas and she was still taking O-levels, like a fairy tale Princess, condemned to complete an impossible task — or else...And two years later she was still at it.

Arnold Arnold's mother had a difficult time during her pregnancy, and so did he for he had to share her pelvis with a large ovarian cyst. After a difficult delivery he arrived two weeks late, weighing 5 lbs and needing special nursing. But he managed to pass all his landmarks without trouble or marked delay, and at his junior school was said to do well, except that he did not learn to read despite one year's extra remedial help. This was continued at his comprehensive school, where he was lucky enough to be taught three times a week by a highly skilled teacher sent by the Education Authority. Her report, which accompanied him on his visit to the Clinic at the age of 16 years 4 months, described him as strongly motivated to learn, able to hold his own in maths and technical drawing, but with both auditory discrimination and recall equally poor. His only way of making even small advances in reading had been through frequent and patient repetition of the building-up process.

The Clinic staff found him a mature, pleasant, co-operative lad, glad of the opportunity to discuss his areas of difficulty and talent, of which he was well aware, and looking for help in planning his future. His mother wanted him to take seven subjects at CSE, his school had offered to keep him an extra year, and he wanted to be a post office engineer. Tests showed all his auditory skills to be slightly below average. His comprehension when reading orally was that of a seven-year-old, when reading silently a little higher, with average intelligence and good manual dexterity. Since he was unlikely to enter, unaided, into his preferred occupation, the Clinic immediately appealed to the Careers Service and the Employment Medical Advisory Service. The latter suggested that he might in due course, and if still unemployed, be taken on by a Skill Centre. However, after sitting his seven CSE exams he took matters into his own hands: he found himself a job as a handyman in a block of offices and left school.

This is not as unhopeful a case as might at first appear, for a significant number of lads like Arnold, having reached the age of 21 or 22, seek out help in adult literacy classes. These provide situation-orientated tuition. Once freed from the failure of school reading tests, which are irrelevant outside school, and with a clearly defined and limited objective some reading success generally follows. Even the old basic literacy skills from the Clinic list given below are approached selectively and the necessary ones, if not already acquired, are now brushed up. Without becoming readers in the accepted sense of the word, they can get by confidently, even with a slim safety margin. A literate marriage partner, with both self-employed in the same small business, often results in a prosperous and successful partnership. The compulsory civic duty of jury service, once the hurdle of oath-taking has been negotiated reveals such people, according to one judge, to be clear-headed, with retentive memory for events, and brisk evaluation of character — so long as no case involving documents comes their way.

Check List of Basic Literacy Skills

This list contains a number of items which, it is suggested, all school leavers should be able to read/know about/use/write. Some of the items will be learnt and used very much earlier and more often than others, some are intended to bridge the gap between the non-reader and the functional reader, a very few are intended to provide general background information.

Obviously the list is neither exhaustive nor final: indeed it cannot be either, for each individual will add to it a few items of vital importance to himself, and drop others which are of no concern to him. For instance understanding of the London underground map is of limited use to school leavers at large.

The items have been divided into three groups, according to the frequency with which they are likely to be used, and labelled with three stars for the most urgent, and a decreasing number of stars denoting decreasing urgency. This classification will probably also vary with the needs of the individual.

***	**	*
1 own signature 2 own full name in capitals		

	***	**	*
3	(a) home address in capitals	(b) home address spaced as on envelope	
4	school/work address in capitals		
5	date of birth (digits only)		
6	actual date (digits only)		
7	phone number (digits only)		
8	days of the week (a) read (b) say in sequence		days of the week (c) write
9	months (a) read (b) say in sequence		months (c) write
10		seasons (a) read (b) say in sequence (c) relate seasons to months	seasons (d) write
11	tell the time		
12	tell left and right (a) on self (b) in room	tell left and right (c) on another person	
13	(a) know name and address of next of kin		(b) write name and address of next of kin
14	use of 999		
15	use of telephone (a) private (b) public (c) via operator		
16		say alphabet in sequence	
17		use of dictionary	
18		use of telephone directory	
19		use of calendar	
20			know names of: (a) own local authority (b) 4 cardinal points

	***	**	*
21	know location of nearest: (a) telephone (b) GPO (c) doctor (d) chemist (e) police station (f) town hall		
22		use of altas/map/ street map	
23		use of atlas index	
24		use of underground map	
25		understand road signs and safety signs at work	
26			point on map to: (a) U.K. (b) London (c) own home town (d) EEC countries (e) 5 continents (f) 7 oceans
27	recognise coinage		
28	give change for up to £5		
29	read (a) essential notices (b) 50 address words (c) 50 job advert words		
30		read 100 commonest words (a) 1st group 12 (b) 2nd group 20 (c) 3rd group 68	
31			find standard items in newspaper (e.g. sport, TV)
32		read words for (a) common colours (b) numbers 1 — 20	
33			know about (a) voting procedures (b) jury service (c) rights of the arrested

Teachers may also like to use some of the following books and materials.

Authors	**Titles**	**Publishers***
Bill Ridgway	*Read All About It*	Edward Arnold
	What's All This About?	Edward Arnold
	Words About Town	Edward Arnold
	Words About the House	Edward Arnold
H. M. Dobinson	*Basic Skills You Need*	Nelson
M. W. Thomas	*Managing Your Money* (In Focus Books)	Nelson
A. G. Akers and G. L. Booth	*Your Wage Packet* (On Your Own Books)	Nelson
	Your Holiday (On Your Own Books)	Nelson
	Your Bank Account (On Your Own Books)	Nelson
A. Hanson	*Ready to Leave* (pupils' workbook)	Collins
W. K. Brennan	*School Leavers' Work Tasks and Handbook*	E. J. Arnold
Home Office Unit	*Key to Form Filling*	Macmillan
Home Office Unit	*Applying for a New Job*	Macmillan
British Standards Institution and Consumers' Association	*Dangers and Disasters: A consumer education pack on safety*	Department of Prices and Consumer Protection

The following will help to teach some items from the Check List on pages 77.

Items	**Materials**	**Made by/From***
8 and 9	*Calendar Vocabulary Flash Cards*	Philip and Tacey
11	*Round the Clock Jigsaw*	Galt
	Clock	Galt
16	*Alphabet Pattern Plaques*	Galt
24	*The London Game*	Hi Toys (England)/ Hamleys
26 (a), (b), (c)	*England and Wales Jigsaw*	Galt
	Great Britain: Industrial Life	Victory Jigsaw/ Hamleys
	Great Game of Britain	Hi Toys

*Addresses will be found on page 139.

		(England)/ Hamleys
26 (d), (e), (f)	*The World Jigsaw, Europe Jigsaw*	Victory Jigsaw/ Hamleys
	'Go'	Waddington/ Hamleys
29 (a)	*Essential Notices Flash Cards*	Philip and Tacey
	Key Words for Social Competency (about 400)	Peter Daffon Associates
	Key Words for Following Instructions (about 700) (both for older readers)	Peter Daffon Associates
	Quin Reading Games	Cressrelles
29 (b), 30	*Quin Reading Games*	Cressrelles
	English Sign Language (by M. R. Pearce)	Harrap

More on language

With this spectrum of overlapping difficulties the teacher may well wonder where to start. The following suggestions, based on personal preference, are made on the strict understanding that the list does not try to be exhaustive and concentrates on the area which, from conversations with teachers, is thought to be the least familiar one. Most of the items mentioned can be examined with the help of publishers' arrangements for inspection copies, at special exhibitions, at the Centre for Language in Primary Education and the Diagnostic Centre, both housed at the Ebury Teachers' Centre, Sutherland Street, London SW1, and at ILEA's Education Equipment Centre, 275 Kennington Lane, London SE11. The last is open throughout the year. Neither is limited to ILEA teachers.

Young's Oral *Verbal Intelligence Test*[1] will give the class teacher an indication of the general level of language development of his pupils. It is easy to administer to groups and quick to score, suitable from age 7 years 6 months.

The *English Picture Vocabulary Test* is a much easier test, again speedy to administer to groups and mark and suitable in its various stages for ages 3 to adult. Pupils enjoy doing it.

Both these tests have their legitimate critics, but remain serviceable. For an informal but illuminating assessment, done with small groups, it is

[1] Publishers of items recommended in this section are listed on pages 139.

possible to make use of graded language structures in the order of their introduction in a scheme for teaching English as a foreign language such as Geoffrey Broughton's *Success with English.* One of the many advantages of this and other similar schemes, such as *Target,* is that they include taped material so that listening skills and oracy are practised as well as written language.

Without benefit of tape recorders younger children and teachers greatly enjoy and pupils learn by stealth from *Okki-tokki-unga* (action songs), and Clive Sanson's *Speech Rhymes, Acting Rhymes, Counting Rhymes* and *Rhythm Rhymes.*

Quin's *Reading Games* include two bingo-type games, one of rhymes and one of auditory discrimination of consonant blends and clusters.

The up-to-date catalogues of Learning Development Aids (LDA) and Remedial Supply Company deserve the closest attention. The latter has graded oral exercises, starting with absolute basics and rising to levels where written answers to oral questions are needed. LDA's *Learning to Listen, Sound Lotto* and *Sound Stories* cover the earlier stages in greater detail.

DLM Auditory Motor Program consists of a series of eight-minute tapes, giving instructions to follow on worksheets. It is good for learning names of colours, for position in space, letter names, and so on, and is distributed in the UK by Taskmaster Ltd (see page 139).

From E. J. Arnold there is *Concept 7-9,* devised by the Schools Council as one of its language projects, and an excellent mix of tapes, activity books, named cards, and other materials, good for vocabulary extension and verbal reasoning on the basis of pictorial information. Unit 1, *Listening with Understanding,* suitable for six-year-olds, covers a comparable order of difficulty to DLM.

ILEA's *Language for Learning – Listen, discuss and do* is suitable for ages six upwards. This is attractive for the variety of tasks to be performed. Longman have a number of taped materials suitable for older pupils, listed in their 'Ways to English' catalogue. In particular *Listening Comprehension* Part 2a contains aural comprehension passages. The accompanying workbook includes many multiple choice questions. Some of the *Longman Structural Readers* are on tape, with questions including reproduction, and an answer book. Similarly, some of the *Knockouts* series are taped, so that the texts can be followed, or used for paired reading, but comprehension questions would have to be added to these entertaining stories for secondary level pupils. For pupils needing more sophisticated material any of the Talking Books could be adapted with the addition of comprehension exercises.

When it comes to speech there is a lot to be said for starting with 'talking through' games of visual discrimination, and continuing in this way with gradually more complicated games including verbal reasoning for any game on the 'Happy Families' principle. Sequential concept thinking cards are very useful and several houses publish them. LDA have the precisely targeted *Why Because* cards and the open-ended *Concept Snap,* a good game at any level of sophistication, although older and more ingenious players may need an adjudicator.

Any programmes, kits, books designed to stimulate written work, such as *Write Again,* can be used, but with a tape recorder rather than paper. *Write Again* (for secondary pupils) lends itself particularly to this treatment because the start of the story, which is given and broken off at a cliff-hanger, can be recorded first as a lead in for the pupil who will complete it.

When it comes to written comprehension the range of commercially available materials is enormous and teachers add their own exercises to available texts. Two thoroughly reliable series, which have the extra merit of leading from one to the other, are *Reading to Some Purpose* and *Directions — Reading Skills.* It is to be hoped that *Directions,* at present consisting of two books only, will be expanded particularly with cloze and sequencing exercises. Even before the publication of Lunzer and Gardner's *Effective Use of Reading* (1979) teachers have known the particular value of these two types of exercises, and a few examples of each are to be found in *Directions.*

Cloze exercises consist of passages from which — generally — every tenth word has been deleted and the pupil has to supply it. This serves to bring to the forefront of his consciousness his subconscious and automatic knowledge of language structures. The text has to provide cues to the gaps, the cues working either forward or backward, directing the attention either to the meaning of a particular word in the context of the passage (that is, emphasising the ideas expressed) or the syntactical connection (how the ideas progress). Teachers making their own cloze exercises will know that it takes much longer to write one from scratch than to use an extant text with slight adaptations. The specially-made ones are likely to be more precisely targeted. The temptation is to put all the missing words in a list at the top, but this alters the nature of the exercise. On the other hand straight comprehension questions at the end are useful in extracting the important points from the passage.

The passage below is quite difficult to read but, bar one gap, very easy to complete.

> In the 18th century the Turkish empire stretched over ____________ large part of present day Yugoslavia. At that time ____________ the villages of the province called Serbia, there was ____________ formal education for all children. But children derived knowledge ____________ historical and current events from songs. Anybody could

recite __________ sing them, or compose them. New songs were circulated __________ one village to the next by blind men, travellers __________ outlaws. The blind men were the specialists, going round __________ houses in a district, singing a song in __________ of each and begging. After a gift had __________ given they would sing again. On holy days they __________ outside churches and monasteries. Travellers on the other hand __________ expected to part-pay for their lodging by singing songs __________ to their hosts. Finally outlaws lying up for the __________ in friendly houses sang songs about other outlaws. All __________ groups sang of exploits against the Turks.

The second passage is easier to read but has every seventh word omitted. This obviously makes the completion process more difficult.

The invention of glass making is __________ credited to the Phoenicians. Basically glass __________ made of sand which is fused __________ soda and lime. Soda was taken __________ seaweed and plants which grew profusely __________ the shores and estuaries of Phoenicia. The Phoenicians being adventurous sailors, glass was __________ to all Mediterranean ports. In __________ early times glass was used for __________ because glass mixtures could be coloured __________ if used to coat small objects, __________ them look like precious stones. Another __________ with the coloured glass mixture was __________ pour it into moulds made of __________ or metal and shaped like tiny __________ or ornaments. If a hollow object __________ wanted the glass mixture was applied __________ the outside of the moulds which were easily broken later.

The specifically targeted passage below was designed for a boy in the last term of junior school. He had very good oracy, poor spelling and considerable ability as an actor. He was encouraged to use discussion and a dictionary in order to complete the phonically-based exercise which was intended to:

(a) direct his attention to words with -mp-, a consonant blend from which, in free writing, he generally omitted the 'm';

(b) remind him that the -ed ending of verbs could indicate either the narrative past tense or the passive form (not that these terms had been used when the point had originally been drawn to his attention);

(c) remind him of the difference between plain adjective, its comparative form, its adverb, the spellings of the last two, and the uses of all three (for instance, the use of 'than' implies a comparison);

(d) make him think of the possible semantic content of the deletions and find their equivalent among the listed words (most of which he knew the meaning of);

(*e*) improve his command of vocabulary by teaching him some new words and consolidating his hold of those of which he had half forgotten the meaning.

Fill the blanks with the words in the box below, and then read the story aloud — beautifully:

ample	crumpets	umpteen	grumpy	damply
hump	frumpish	lamp	limpets	bumpier
simple	dump	empty	sumptuous	glimpsed
rubbish-dump		rumpled	lumped	camping

After the autumn storms the steep road to the __________ site was __________ than I remembered it. The rain-soaked site looked quite __________ as I parked the van in front of the __________ club-house, its windows gleaming __________ in the __________-light. Between it and the sea, darker than the cloudy sky, was the great rock, arched smoothly like a __________-backed whale, its cover of sea-weed and __________ growing again after the scouring of __________ feet throughout the summer. But was it quite undisturbed? A sudden gleam of the faltering sun gave __________ light to see a strange figure, covered in a shapeless garment, __________ by the freshening wind. He, or she, for I could not tell its gender, was hopping off the rock and towards the shrubs screening the rubbish-__________ I followed, calling, but the wind __________ my words into a meaningless gust and carried them out to sea. I pushed through the prickly holm-oaks, and there as expected, was the __________-__________, a rectangle of derelict plastic and aerosols. But on the far side of it, dwarfing the wind-blown tamarisks and bare olives, was a __________ tent, dazzlingly coloured, like a picture in a fairy tale. Outside it was the __________ figure, first __________ on the rock. The voice was hoarse, the tone __________, and the message brief: 'No __________ for tea.'

On first reading he inserted, correctly, *camping, lamp, hump, dump, rubbish-dump* and *crumpets.* The second reading added *bumpier, damply, limpets, umpteen, sumptuous, frumpish* and *grumpy.* The third deletion, requiring *empty,* took a long while, because it is covered by a backward-working cue about half-way through the passage. The exercise took him about half an hour.

Sequencing exercises in the form of jumbled sentences ('they for do us what take') are familiar from the easiest of reading and spelling books. Next come jumbled stories, with sentences in an *ad hoc* order. Sorting these out is analogous to sorting out pictorial sequential thinking concept cards. Finally there should be many texts with jumbled paragraphs — that is, exercises in sequencing larger units of meaning. Teachers often tackle this from the other end when trying to teach essay construction. Arguably inchoate essays would be thinner on the ground if more of the last sequencing exercises were easily available.

Summarising exercises are fortunately common in books for all age groups, inference questions slightly less so, but these are very easy to add to reading texts.

The choice of these faces teachers with the usual arguments about the experience of literature for pupils with limited reading ability and even less stamina for it. Is there to be a search for a well-written book, short enough and of readability level suitable for these pupils' attainments, or should an abbreviated version of the classics be sought? Classics, apart from constant availability in various degrees of faithfulness to the original, have two advantages, a good story line and access to the national mythology, important for pupils who are otherwise unlikely to find out what Man Friday, Lilliput, Captain Nemo and even 007 refer to.

Authors	*Titles*	*Publishers**
D. Young	*Oral Verbal Intelligence Test*	Hodder and Stoughton
M. A. Brimer and L. M. Dunn	*English Picture Vocabulary Tests*	Educational Evaluation Enterprises
G. Broughton (editor)	*Success with English* series	Penguin Books
L. G. Alexander, J. Tadman and R. H. Kinsbury	*Target* series	Longman
B. Harrop (editor)	*Okki-tokki-unga* (action songs for children)	A. and C. Black
C. Sansom	*Speech Rhymes*	A. and C. Black
	Acting Rhymes	A. and C. Black
	Counting Rhymes	A. and C. Black
	Rhythm Rhymes	A. and C. Black
V. Quin	*Quin Reading Games*	Cressrelles
LDA	*Learning to Listen*	Learning Development Aids
	Sound Lotto	Learning Development Aids

LDA	*Sound Stories*	Learning Development Aids
	Why Because Cards	Learning Development Aids
	Concept Snap	Learning Development Aids
J. Wight (Project Director)	*Concept 7 to 9*	E. J. Arnold for Schools Council
ILEA	*Language for Learning: Unit 4 — Listen, discuss and do*	ILEA Learning Materials Service
D. Byrne	*Listening Comprehension*	Longman
W. S. Allen (editor)	*Structural Readers* series	Longman
J. Levine (editor)	*Knockouts*	Longman
R. Edwards	*Write Again*	Macmillan Educational
P. Flowerdew and R. Ridout	*Reading to Some Purpose*	Oliver and Boyd
J. Cooper	*Directions — Reading Skills*	Oliver and Boyd
E. A. Lunzer and K. Gardner	*The Effective Use of Reading*	Heinemann Educational

Abbreviated versions of the classics are to be found in several series, for example *Oxford Progressive English Readers* (Oxford University Press), *Bullseye* series (Hutchinson), and four series all published by Longman: *Simplified English* series, *Structural Readers* series, *Squirrels,* and *Bridge* series.

* Addresses will be found on page 139.

6
Vision

The human visual system plays such an important part in the development of a child's awareness of his environment, and of those basic skills necessary for classroom success, that some consideration of the anatomy, physiology, development and what may go wrong with the eye is warranted here.

Light enters through a translucent curved window, the cornea, is rationed by the contraction or dilation of the pupil according to its intensity, and is then focused by the lens on to the retina. This is a thin cellular sheet of about 100 million rods which are sensitive to light and shade, and 5-6 million cones which are sensitive to colour. These are the receptor

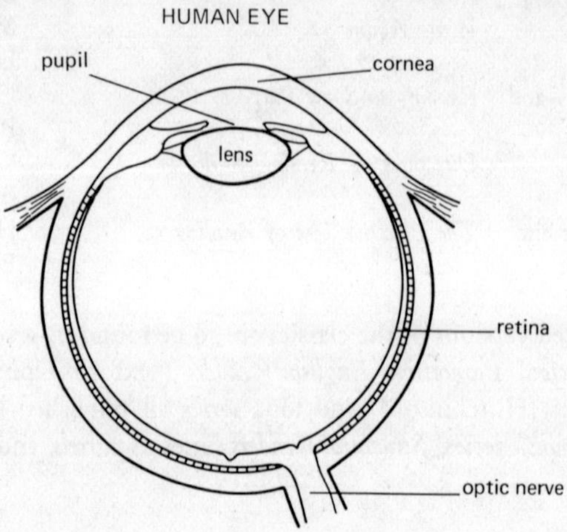

Figure 7 *Horizontal section of the left human eye.*

cells of the visual system which turn light energy into nerve impulses. They do no communicate directly with the brain, but make synapses (connections) with secondary neurons (main nerve cells), which in turn communicate with ganglion cells. The axons (long ultra-gossamer fibres emanating from main nerve cells) of these join together to form the optic nerve. The fibres of the optic nerve pass to an intermediate relay station, and from there to the visual areas of the cerebral hemispheres.

The organisation of the visual cortex is complex. Between the retina and the brain, half the fibres in the optic nerve of one eye cross over to join half the fibres of the other. As a result those portions of the visual fields of both eyes concerned with the right side of the body reach the left side of the brain, while those from the left side reach the right. Both eyes are therefore represented in both halves of the cerebrum.

The retina is accurately mapped in the cortex, so that destruction of a small part of brain causes a corresponding loss of that area of visual field which it reflects. Each point on the retina is represented by a column of cells, running from the surface to the underlying core of white matter. There are three types of cell in each column: simple, complex and hypercomplex, distinguishable by the stimuli which excite them.

Simple cells respond to light falling on a particular spot on the retina. Complex cells are stimulated by contrasting light and shade running in a specific axis, some responding to horizontal lines and others to vertical ones. In both cases the stimuli must move if the cell is to be activated. The hypercomplex cells react to even more complicated stimuli of movements and alignments in relation to the retina. Cortical cells need specific information before they can pass on a message, and there is a hierarchy of selectivity amongst them, which enables patterns to be seen by the cortex. The interpretation of what has been seen is visual perception, necessarily learnt from past visual experiences.

There are two eyes, each receiving information: vision is binocular, an arrangement which enables us to see in depth, but which requires some underlying mechanisms. There must be an ability to see two images at the same time, one from each retina, which the brain must correlate and either superimpose or blend together. There must also be an ability to see two slightly different images, one on each retina, so that when a solid object is viewed, an idea of its depth can be obtained from the two images.

Objects, targets, the things we want to look at, do not stand still and neither do we, so pursuit movements by the eyes are necessary. In order to maintain the integrity of binocular vision while following a moving object, coordination of the six muscles of each eye is required. This ensures that the sensitive area of the retina remains beamed on to the target. If the object is approaching or receding, eyes must converge or diverge, while the lens, by changing shape, must alter its focal length so that the target is kept in view and in focus. This pre-supposes that we know what we want to look at. The position is different for the tiny baby, who has not had experience of his environment.

There are some differences between the new born child's eye and that of the adult. The former is smaller, though the cornea is relatively large. The sensitive central area of the retina is poorly developed, the balance between the muscles is weak and visual perception is poor. Fixation on an object can occur (that is, the baby can stare at something), but at other times the eyes tend to move around independently of each other, giving the appearance of a squint.

At three months old the eyes work in harness, fixing on an object moving across the line of sight. Switching from one target to another may occur. Moving objects coming towards the child can be watched as they get closer. The relationship between what can be felt and what can be seen is beginning so that, by exploration of the environment using both sight and touch, the differences between things seen may be learnt and stored in the memory.

By a year the permanence of things is recognised, it is no longer necessary to re-explore previously seen objects when they reappear, memory serves as a short cut.

By two years of age, things are labelled, language and vision are combined. By five or six a child's perception resembles that of an adult, though the relationship of one component to another in a whole may not be properly recognised; for instance, the letters in a word may be known, but their exact position in the word is not identified.

Eye movements play an important role in the development of visual perception. Three types will be mentioned:

1 Pursuit movements are those used to follow a moving object. The accuracy and precision of these movements improves chiefly between the ages of six and eleven, when there is still some slight development to take place.
2 Saccadic movements consist of the movement of the eye from one target to another, and carry out a searching, checking role, flickering the most sensitive reception area of the retina around the object viewed. Shapes are explored by rapid looking, 'stroking' the object with little flashes of sight. The capability of checking and recognising shapes hidden among similar ones increases until the age of six. Once learnt, the shape of an object does not need to be rechecked with saccadic movements.
3 In addition the eyes make minute movements which keep the image of an object moving on the retina and therefore provide the stimulation necessary to make the simple and complex cells of the cerebral cortex respond.

The eye movements which aid in the scanning of the fields of vision for things to look at also help to identify and reconnoitre the shape of targets. Without this identification the reproduction of shapes is impossible.

The perception of space occurs in the presence of objects, as Piaget has pointed out. It develops more rapidly than the conception of space; imagination lags behind facts. Obviously many things may interfere with the visual system and therefore with development of perception and conception of space.

The passage of light from outside on to the retina may be interrupted or distorted. If the curve of the cornea is abnormal (that is, astigmatic), the image thrown on the retina is blurred. If the lens is not clear due to cataract, which occurs rarely in young children, the light is fragmented as though it had passed through a starred window. If the eyeball is too long and the lens cannot accommodate sufficiently, then the image will fall short of the retina; the converse occurs if the eyeball is too short, as in myopia (short sight).

The effect of faulty peripheral vision is not a potent factor in the reproduction of reading problems in children, in fact, there is a higher incidence of myopes (shortsighted children) amongst clever children than amongst the academically unsuccessful. Short sight, which often becomes apparent just before or during early school years, is not brought on by overuse of the eye, by too much reading or by burying the nose in a book. However, blindness or partial blindness are associated with additional disabilities and symptoms, amongst which are language and speech problems, excessive speech to make up for loss of vision and a variety of behavioural problems not found in other stressful and exacting situations.

If it is easy for the teacher to spot the child with his head on his arm and his eye too close to the page, it is often as easy to recognise the cross-eyed child. A squint is present when one eye looks at an object and the other does not. The muscle imbalance causing the squint can be congenital or acquired. Three main groups of factors may cause a squint:

1 *sensory* — something may interfere with the proper formation of a retinal image;
2 *motor* — there may be something wrong with the eye muscles or the nerves controlling them;
3 *central* — there may be a general physical or mental illness, combined with a low IQ.

All squints must be referred to an eye specialist for diagnosis and treatment as soon as they are recognised and, for the child's sake, it is always worth risking a snub from the parents, 'Yes, of course we have done something about it.'

Training programmes have been devised which involve the use of eye movements designed to 'exercise' the eyes. The aim is to improve coordination of the eyes, so that the child is taught the required visual and perceptive habits. Some authorities such as Goldberg and Schiffman regard these exercises as useless, except for the increased motivation of the patient as a result of increased attention and understanding. The eye movements of adults reading their own language, compared to the eye movements of the same people attempting to read an unfamiliar language, are quoted as evidence that faulty eye movements are the result and not the cause of learning problems, nullifying any rationale for trying to correct them.

The situation is different with regard to visual perception which is itself learnt. However, the development of visual perception should, as has been mentioned above, be completed by early school years and the recognition of perceptual handicaps should be made before the age of six, so that remediation may take place. There are children who lag behind after this age and they are to some extent helped by remedial work, such as the Frostig programme, directed at increasing perception. It is perhaps significant that in the Clinic dealing with school age children visual perceptual problems are relatively rare compared to language ones; on the other hand, in a neighbouring unit dealing with much younger children the reverse is true. Language development is affected by faulty visual perception or conception, so that in the classroom the presenting symptom of failure to read or spell shows as a facet of language, but the difficulty in finding five hidden starfish in a seaside picture, or a lack of interest in train spotting, may not be recognised as important.

In practical terms the principal visual perceptual skills should have developed by the age of six and failure to conform to this developmental pattern may mean that there is a failure to develop fully the association between letters and sounds. Problems with recognising the difference between confusable letters such as 'b' and 'd' take the longest to resolve, but should have been overcome by eight. Children younger than eight often develop strategems to cope with their difficulty, the simplest being the substitution of capital letters for lower case as the former have greater individuality of shape — 'B' does not resemble 'D' to the same extent as 'b' does 'd'. When writing letters the bright child may capitalise on his intelligence in this way.

Testing for visual perceptual defects amongst older school children often yields poor results, serving to identify not so much the defect as its after effects, which may be poor memory for sequences, poor coding ability, or a poor linkage between sound and shape.

Why visual perception should develop poorly is not always known; however, a strong body of opinion believes it to be associated in some cases with the same sort of brain damage occurring during the vulnerable period around birth as can affect coordination. As long as there is no complicating weakness, and given the appropriate pre-school help, there seems to be a fair chance of improvement taking place.

Visual experience is inextricably entwined with language development. What has been seen must be remembered and stored both as a visual impression and as a language symbol. It is impossible to recall what has not been experienced. Take, for example, Fielding's comment that it must be absurd to discourse on colours with a man born blind. He quotes such a one who 'entertained of the colour scarlet, that colour seemed very much like the sound of a trumpet.' The whole field of visual memory is enormously broad, covering a range from short-term 'immediate' traces to long-term stores where linguistic and visual information seem to become one and the same. If the development of visual perception is delayed so will be the development of language dependent on it. If the visual system is altered or damaged so will be the semantic memory which is formed from the synthesis of sensations.

Obviously a considerable variety of clinical pictures may originate in alterations from the normal pattern of development. However, the Clinic experience has been that three types of case occur more frequently than others. Firstly there are the children with clear cut visual perceptual problems who are on the whole young and have not developed strategies to circumvent their difficulties. Secondly, there are the children who present as 'phonic' spellers supporting an apparently inadequate visual component of memory by overemphatic use of the auditory channel. Thirdly, there are the children who present as 'bizarre' spellers and seem unable to recall both the sight and the sound pattern of words which they wish to spell.

The cases described below present some of the problems encountered in this field.

Benjamin There seemed to be no reason why Benjamin, a tubby tow-haired little boy, should be in trouble at school. After his mother's normal pregnancy and delivery, together with his uneventful childhood and secure family background, it was a surprise to everyone that he should be 'difficult to settle down to work' and 'failing' at reading. His IQ was revealing: the verbal portion was in the 'very superior' category, the performance portion was only 'bright normal', a score which many of us would be glad of for our children, but not when compared to the first. He was very articulate on the frustrations of not being able to 'write stories', or read to himself easily the stories about Paddington Bear, despite a reading age of 8 years 8 months, when his chronological age was 7 years 9 months. His spelling was a little worse. However, he had well-defined perceptual difficulties with copying patterns, sorting out objects from a patterned background and spatial relationships in two dimensions. He had no difficulty in short-term visual sequential memory. After using the appropriate sections of the Frostig training programme (plus games to be played informally at home) for seven months, the figure ground weakness improved; with it there was a quite remarkable jump in his reading comprehension. In seven months of elapsed time his comprehension score had improved by 21 months, being now consistent with his verbal IQ, and his spelling was level with his chronological age. Significantly his spelling miscues now consisted of reasonable phonic alternatives, such as would be expected in his age group, rather than mistakes in letter order and *ad hoc* insertions and ommissions which had characterised his earlier efforts.

Barbara During pregnancy Barbara's mother was found to be Rhesus negative, which caused some anxiety and more when, just before the birth, she was unconscious for 24 hours for no discovered reason. However labour and birth were normal and Barbara seemed well on arrival, but initially she did not thrive and was restless and wakeful at night. A squint became evident at eighteen months and she was given glasses to correct it. Her mother was always worried about her, though walking, talking and toilet training went smoothly. At an early age she was managing her mother; each mealtime she refused to eat what was put in front of her and insisted, successfully, on having something else cooked for her between meals, her mother being afraid that she would starve if she went without. Every night she woke her mother for a drink, though she had a night light and could quite well have helped herself. Every morning Barbara rejected the clothes that her mother had laid out for her, because Barbara wanted to look like her mates and her mother wanted her to look pretty. Jeans versus frillies — jeans won.

When she started school she was thought to be bright and all went well at first, but she began to develop attacks of vomiting. These scared her mother, until it was recognised that they only occurred when her best friend, who helped her with lessons, was away.

When seen at the Clinic at the age of 7 years 4 months she was markedly cross-eyed, but very pretty, with glasses that were the height of fashion. She coped much better with what she heard than with what she saw, though this was not due to any problem with visual acuity. She could see all right, but had difficulty in interpreting what she saw. This was reflected in her IQ results: there was a 39-point difference between her 'bright normal' verbal intelligence and her borderline performance one. More particularly, her verbal reasoning was in the 'superior' range, whilst she was confused by a coding test, had difficulty in visual scanning, and was utterly defeated by a simple jigsaw. With much care, she put the pieces together, one edge matching one edge only, but nothing fitting and at one stage she placed one piece on top of another with great precision. She had no idea of number, recognised the words *a, up, to, my, I* and *in;* knew reliably the name and sound of the letters 'O' and 'S', and could not read. She was particularly confused visually over 'b' and 'd', 'f' and 't', 'm' and 'w', 'j' and 'g', 'v' and 'y'. An electro-encephalogram showed minimal abnormality in the left temporal region.

At the case conference the recommendations were unanimous: a great deal of visual work, directed by an occupational therapist, and all of it accompanied by a verbal self-monitoring commentary; a strictly phonic approach to reading; at home a considerable number of informal games and activities that would involve visual and tactile discrimination, again with commentary. Home, school and special tutor would have to cooperate closely.

She was admitted to a small once weekly reading group and started as a very self-contained, silent little girl, who worked with determination, gave no smiles, and only whispered when spoken to. The occupational therapist in attendance gave her a progression of visual exercises. When it came to letter shapes Barbara was persuaded to lie on the floor forming the shapes, then to crawl and later walk through the letter shapes always facing in the same direction, so that at times she had to walk backwards or sideways. For a change from the occupational therapist, the speech therapist was asked to ensure that she knew and was able to demonstrate the meanings of fifty common words and phrases for position in space and start on number work with the help of tactile stimuli. A phonic reading scheme with particularly uncluttered illustrations was chosen: *Linguistic Readers* by C. G. Stratemeyer and H.L. Smith (Nisbet).

The occupational therapist and the social worker went to visit the family, to explain the nature of the disability and suggest helpful games and domestic activities, such as laying the table, sorting the vegetables into separate containers, measuring out the ingredients and making a cake, stamping out pastry. With a charming giggle Barbara's mother declared herself a 'rotten manager', said she would never dream of making a cake or biscuits, or of buying loose vegetables, and refused the offer of additional occupational therapy in the holidays. The remedial teacher went to Barbara's school, where she had indeed been having daily remedial tuition on a phonic basis for a year. However, without the preliminary visual work and no phonic reading scheme (Barbara was allowed to choose any one of a large selection of loosely grouped books) the remedial tuition had shown no result. A parcel of teaching materials, including phonic texts, was handed over, and school and reading group were able to teach in parallel.

Six months later, in the course of the Illinois Test of Psycholinguistic Ability (ITPA), the clinical psychologist found, without surprise, that on every pair of tests, visual test scores were significantly below auditory ones, with visual association and visual memory specifically deficient skills. But she knew her left from her right on herself, and no longer rotated or inverted any letters. She was able to cope with several different board games and in particular could recognise whether numbers up to 100 'went up or down'. On the other hand she had to pause before knowing what numbers showed on the dice she had thrown.

Another six months later, that is one year after first attending the Clinic, at the age of 8 years 8 months she knew reliably the names and sounds of all single letters of the alphabet, consonant blends, the digraphs 'sh', 'th', 'ch', 'oo', 'ee', 'ar', 'er', 'all', 'oi' and 'oy' giving her a reading age of nearly eight. She was much less shy, her voice was habitually audible and she even occasionally raised it in indignation at the bigger boys. Then one day she didn't turn up. School had not seen her either. Telephone calls, letters, enquiries — no reply. She seemed to have vanished in a puff of phonics.

We *would* like to know how she got on.

Phonic spelling

'A pqulere shape was aproching from the sutherne vaileye gradguhly they distingwisht an aroplane sercoling above.'

If language is the symbolisation of thought, then there is nothing wrong with that sentence, since the symbols used, being reasonable phonic alternatives, adequately convey the thought. When seen for the first time it may even amuse, as well as inform, but class teachers will recognise that the pupil who spells like that presents a consistent picture.

He will be of bright or of average intelligence, with normal receptive and expressive speech, so that he fully understands what is said to him and orally can make himself fully understood. If asked to read out aloud, he can be seen, and sometimes heard, to sound out words as he reads. After puberty, he will tend to rush at reading, snatching at contextual clues and losing accuracy, if not the gist of the text. His visual sequential memory (that is, the ability to recall the correct order of shapes seen) will be that of a much younger child. This type of memory is measured by the ITPA subtest which has a cut-off point at 10 years 5 months (see page 5), and it is possible to identify the age below this ceiling which development has reached. It is as though there is difficulty holding the order of letters in the mind's eye, until a check on the familiarity of the sequence has been made at the memory store. If the picture of the sequence fades too rapidly, the word has to be re-read, or sound clues brought in to assist in recognition. The difficulty lies in checking the visual presentation of the word with stored memory of the word held in the private dictionary, which in these cases is limited like that of a much younger child.

In the classroom several things happen: the pupil's slow ponderous reading aloud excites ridicule from the rest of the class; anything written on the board by the teacher may be wiped off before there has been time to read it; all written work is covered with corrections made initially by the pupil and then by the teacher, and is often marked down for poor spelling rather than poor content; foreign languages, such as French, can be learnt orally, but as the phonic clues are so different from the well-known English ones spelling is even more of a disaster. Latin, giving access to the meaning and spelling of so many words outside the range of reading schemes, is taught in a minority of schools, and is usually introduced too late to be of help.

Attempts to learn to spell by copying words over and over again fail, as this hammers away at the skill which is weakest, and the physical stimulus involved in writing of the usual size and with the usual materials is insufficient to stimulate tactile and kinetic memory. The end result can be an anxious, distressed child who spends more time bothering about spelling than about learning and who may give up altogether if the nature of the problem is not identified and accepted. It should be recognised that there is no widely accepted way to speed up the development of visual sequential memory, which improves slowly, but too slowly for academic comfort, whilst the addition of parental- or teacher-induced anxiety will only make matters worse.

Belinda Belinda weighed 10 lbs at birth and was post-mature; her infancy was uneventful and she did quite well at school until she was seven when she was said to be a bad reader but in contrast a good speller. With remedial help this state was reversed, so when she came to the Clinic at the age of eleven she was a good but very slow reader and a bad speller. Her intelligence was in the 'bright normal' range. Her reading comprehension was found to be that of a twelve-year-old and her spelling that of a nine-year-old, her errors being mainly reasonable phonic alternatives. She was given a lot of spelling tuition, being taken systematically through phonic patterns and spelling rules, so that four years later, with her visual sequential memory now normal, her spelling had improved by elapsed time and she was spelling adequately. However, her reading, which was dependent on the amount of reading done generally, for lessons and fun, had not improved. In particular, her silent reading comprehension was significantly below what was expected of her age group.

Belinda was distinctly worried by her overall shortcomings in academic subjects because her obvious rapid grasp of all orally presented topics had placed her firmly in the O-level stream, and she was expected to take eight academic O-levels, including French. With essay writing demanded weekly, her concern with spelling made her neglect the content and planning of written work. It was suggested that she should limit herself to five academic O-levels (dropping French for one), be warned off the English language examination normally taken by her school and directed to one where at least some marks could be obtained on a multiple choice basis, and given early warning how to help herself over history and English literature.

In these circumstances three books were helpful: *English Essay Exercises* by B. Rowe (Hodder and Stoughton); *English at Work*, Book 4B, by T.

Scott (James Brodie); and *Multiple Choice Tests in English Language* by E.L. Black and S.E.F. Finn (John Murray).

Finally Belinda obtained eight O-levels at grades A, B or C, and one CSE grade 1.

Bob In contrast Bob, the boy with the 'pqulere' spelling, had a stormy birth, being a forceps delivery, and was jaundiced for some time after. He weighed 9 lbs 7 oz. Development and health were satisfactory in the early years. Unfortunately he did not enjoy infant school, could not get on with the Initial Teaching Alphabet (ita), was switched to Traditional Orthography and then back again to ita. At seven he was barely able to read. His teachers' attitude was ambivalent: he was thought to be lazy or to have something wrong with his vision, to such an extent that he was more than once referred to a hospital eye department. When first seen in the Clinic at the age of 14 years 6 months he had good expressive language, an excellent vocabulary, good auditory discrimination and attention span. His visual acuity (his ability to see) was normal, so that he could correctly reproduce abstract shapes after seeing them for no more than five seconds. His visual sequential memory was that of a five-year-old and he had little ability to recall the order of letters in words that he wanted to spell.

However, his reading both silent and oral was more than adequate for ordinary purposes, and he was adept at tackling long unfamiliar words by breaking them up into syllables, and monitoring the sense of what he was reading by sensible self-corrections. These techniques had been taught while he was in the remedial stream during the first year of comprehensive school and his progress had raised him out of this bottom group. But his spelling remained grossly below par for the greater academic demands (five academic CSEs) now made upon him. It was suggested that he should be allowed to dictate all written work into a tape recorder and for examinations permission should be sought to use an amanuensis.

This residual weakness in spelling is by far the commonest of the visual deficits that brings children to the Clinic. Reasonable phonic alternatives in the correct order is its mildest form. A less manageable form is the right letters in the wrong order, and up to a point this can be rectified by rigorous auditory monitoring (that is, saying the word to oneself very clearly, exaggerating the component sounds). But even if the slowness and the sheer sweat of this process can be faced, how often is articulation sufficiently good to be useful in this context? In the multi-national schools of the inner cities, where reduced uninflected speech is the rule, this technique cannot be relied on. A better basis is very frequent, carefully structured spelling tuition from the age of six upwards, with regular 'spellings', dictation of complete sentences and frequent attention to wordbuilding, related to handwriting practice. Yet however inspired and meticulous the spelling tuition, it will succeed only if:

the child's difficulty is discovered early;

he is bright and has above average oral language development;

he has a great deal of cheerful support both at home and in school;

the learning programme is geared to immediate visible success to motivate further effort;

the impairment to visual, especially visual sequential, ability as measured by the Illinois Test of Psycholinguistic Ability is within certain tolerance: that is, a score no more than 36 months below that expected for the chronological age (or less than 10 years 5 months for older children).

If the intelligence is below average (below WISC IQ 90) and the oral language development limited to that of a nine-year-old, progress with spelling the extended vocabulary needed for O-levels or high grades at CSE is likely to stick at the 'phonic alternative' stage.

'Bizarre' spelling

As distinct from the child who cannot see a word in his mind's eye and has to use elementary phonics to conjure up some sort of picture on the page, there is the child who cannot hear the tune of the word in the mind's ear and cannot marry the sound to the letters. What he writes may look like words, may even have a sort of syntax, but makes no sense as the 'words' written neither look nor sound like the intended ones. The spelling is 'bizarre', a word used by Sandhya Naidoo (Naidoo 1972) when writing about the spelling of children seen at the Word Blind Centre started in 1966. The existence of this type of spelling will also be known to teachers from Margaret L. Peters' *Diagnostic and Remedial Spelling Manual* (Peters 1975) where the last category of miscues is described as 'unclassifiable.'

Often this symptom is part of a picture of overall failure in literacy subskills, with the single exception of handwriting. In these cases the child will be unable to read except for a very limited number of words recognised on a look and say basis. He will not know the names or the sounds of the individual letters, nor will he be able to identify single letter sounds at the beginning of words. He will be unable to distinguish on the printed page between single letters, words, and sentences, let alone paragraphs. His oral language may be poor. But somehow he will have acquired fluent legible handwriting, generally cursive; if sufficiently extrovert he will be happy to cover pages with random letter sequences, chopped up into *ad hoc* lengths and interspersed with a few of the real words he can read and remember. Such children, from indigenous English-speaking homes, are still occasionally to be found in the last year of junior school.

However the boy described below was both a more complicated and a more hopeful case. His receptive and expressive speech were well developed, he talked clearly and wrote a nice hand — all as might be expected. In addition he read well; only his spelling was catastrophic. The causes of this distinctive disturbance are not established, although Dr Margaret Newton suggests that it arises from inconsistent laterality patterns (Newton 1977). But for practical purposes it can be thought of as a poor ability to associate sounds with the groups of letters which should represent them. Naidoo categorises these children as having difficulty with correlation.

Barnaby Barnaby was aged twelve when he was referred by the School Health Service because nobody, himself included, could understand what he had written. His past history was not very informative. His birth had been uneventful and his early health and development normal, apart from a slight delay in starting to use sentences and some middle ear disease just before he started school at five. He had had to have pus drained from behind the ear drums, a common enough procedure.

At infants' school he was thought to be a late developer and a wait and see policy was adopted. By the time he reached junior school his mother was worried about his lack of progress and, as the school concurred, he was given extra lessons during the games periods and learnt to read from a look and say scheme. When he came to the Clinic he was good at games, in the choir, popular with his contemporaries. He knew that he talked and read well, and to demonstrate the former he gave a short talk on his favourite sport, which was taped, and part of it is repeated here verbatim:

> 'There are lots of moves in fencing, like the lunge, when you hit them on the trunk of the body. But of course your opponent can parry and hit you back. So you've got to make sure that you do hit them and if you miss, then you have got to get back on guard very quickly ... When you go up and down the mat, because you do go up and down and not side to side, only up and down, you have to keep your heels in line. When you go forward, front foot first and back foot — last of course(!) and then the opposite way round for going back.'

Not bad for an off-the-cuff discourse to a strange doctor. He went on to read aloud from his science fiction book which he was reading for fun, and his ability to do so and understand what he had read reflected his chronological age. He then produced his written answers to questions based on homework learnt the night before and done in class that morning.

'Ithe guide pilc and in gersea.'

'The dogs kendly was not mersonfedin the cataloguy.'

'Krites kill kelose kicking hard gusses kendly.'

This impenetrable prose was kept up for a whole sheet of neatly written answers, with one particularly arresting line where all the 'words' were either *the* or began with a 'g' and included another 'g','d' and 'p'. This might have been classified as 'perseveration of rotatable letters' were it not for his well-practised cursive handwriting with all rotatable letters firmly locked into correct position.

On further informal assessment he was found to read on the basis of a considerable sight vocabulary and rapid psycholinguistic guessing which fitted in with his high IQ and eagerness to learn. But phonics had entirely passed him by: he had literally no idea of individual letter sounds, had not grasped the principle of invariable sound-symbol association, he did not know what a rhyme was and he could not remember ever playing games like 'I spy'. In short he seemed never to have analysed words, either visually or auditorily. While the whole word method had worked efficiently to transform the visual-spatial sequence into the auditory-temporal one, it had proved inadequate, in his case, for the reverse process.

The speech therapist gave him a short intensive course in auditory discrimination coupled with letter identification, and his mother was shown how to support this informally by playing related games with him. Some of these are mentioned in the West Sussex County Education Committee Psychological Service pamphlet *Teaching Non-Readers.* The remedial teacher introduced phonics and emphasised spelling rules and slowly his spelling changed from the 'bizarre' to the 'reasonable phonic alternatives'. Despite his very good vocabulary he continued to have difficulty in thinking of rhyming words. Arguably a residual weakness in auditory analysis prevented him from recalling quickly words which are different but share the same sounds. With continued excellent help at school his performance on paper improved and when last heard of he was taking A-levels in maths and physics, having obtained good grades in CSE English and allied subjects.

Significantly his case is one from the early days of the Clinic's operation. A greater emphasis on the integrated approach to reading and writing makes cases like his extremely rare at the time of writing. Thanks to Naidoo and similar writers, teachers have been alerted to the problems signalled by 'bizarre' spelling and start tackling them early. Occasionally when a despondent teenager nearing exams moans that 'My spelling's no good,' and then admits, 'but it used to be terrible, really weird', the

Clinic staff suspect that some teacher has put in many hours of skilled if unobtrusive work.

Fortunately a rarity

Bruce A long time ago a schoolmaster accompanied his pupil to the Clinic, because he said that the boy had a most peculiar problem. Aged eleven and of normal intelligence, he could not spell. To instance the difficulty, the schoolmaster had written out the words 'should, would, fish, shake, shook, hands, things', had asked the boy to learn them that evening and the next morning had dictated them to him as a spelling test. The boy wrote: 'olduhs, uldow, shif, akehs, ookhs, ndsah,ngsiht'. To make things odder, the master said the lad started each word in the middle and put the letters on either side of the first one written, so that the order of writing the letters in 'shake' was e-k-h-a-s.

The lad had an extreme form of a problem which is seen quite often and for which we have no satisfactory answer. These particular children have an overall weakness with sequencing, both sounds and letters. Bruce was a good example of this problem. His mother's pregnancy was for nowadays exceptional, as she was kept in bed for six weeks because of morning sickness and fed on stout to relieve it. His birth was normal, but his speech developed slowly so that by the time he went to school he was difficult to understand and was referred for speech therapy. He had some deafness due to fluid behind the ear drums, but this was drained and he settled down well at school. At the age of ten he was not reading very well, and his parents brought him to the Clinic at the instigation of the family doctor, saying that they wanted to know if he was lazy or had something the matter with him. He had a visual sequential memory of a five-year-old and considerable difficulty with auditory sequencing. He was quite unperturbed, definitely unworried, somewhat indulged by his devoted mother. In view of his double trouble with sequencing, the chances of converting him from a bizarre speller, which he was, to a phonic speller, seemed slim, so that help was focused on improving his comprehension of language and on encouraging the reading out aloud of books which he could manage and which might interest him. The school took an active interest in improving his performance, but in spite of efforts on everyone's part, two years later he was still having trouble with both forms of sequencing and his spelling remained bizarre. (Peculiar was rendered 'pewistconquire'.)

7
Psychiatric Illness

Medical fads and fancies come and go, but the pattern of progress in understanding diseases follows a fairly standard course. A typical case is pulmonary tuberculosis, or consumption. For centuries it was recognised as a low fever, a cough, loss of weight, a wasting away, literally the phthisis of classical times; by the nineteenth century it was also the romantic white death splendidly exploited by Verdi in *La Traviata,* and it retained its symbolic power three-quarters of a century later, when Thomas Mann was writing *The Magic Mountain.* Long before that novel's publication in 1929 science had advanced sufficiently to make identification of bacteria possible. The cause, the tubercle bacillus, was quickly recognised as satisfying Koch's postulates. These are the very backbone of the scientific approach to infectious disease: in lay language, a bug must be collected from an infected animal, grown in a culture and finally shown capable of reproducing the disease in another animal (host). Increasing knowledge of biochemistry and the way the bug works enable the antibiotic cure and the immunising injection to be developed with outstanding success. No longer is it necessary, or even thought necessary, to change the environment from London to a sanatorium half way up a Swiss Alp, and not to eat this or that, for pills and injections do the trick.

The same pattern of events can be recognised in relation to psychiatric illness. First, their names describe the symptoms: anxiety, depression, anorexia nervosa, schizophrenia, without any suggestion of cause or cure. After the description of the cluster of symptoms constituting the disease, causes and mechanisms are sought. Sometimes they are found, depending on the state of advance of science in general, for pharmacology and biochemistry go hand in hand. However, the cure of a psychiatric illness is rarely effective if it is prescribed with much confidence and little reason, the stage when environmental factors receive great emphasis.

Fortunately the biochemists are beginning to map out the complex chemical systems of the brain cells, and drugs which are known to influence those systems are now being used to cure the patient. But the precise patterns of various mental illnesses are not as well defined as, for example, appendicitis or scarlet fever. Therefore cases which to the non-specialist may seem almost exactly alike are treated in a variety of ways. The patient may be talked at, encouraged to talk about himself, be analysed, sympathised with, given pills or shocks, supported, rejected and even locked up for a short time, depending, it would seem, not so much on what is wrong with him, but who is trying to effect the cure.

Understandably a good deal of controversy surrounds the treatment and management of child psychiatric cases. The presentation of material in this chapter expresses one particular view. If the reader disagrees it is as well to remember that a few years' time may prove us both wrong, or even both right.

Depressive disease

To suffer from depressive disease is not the same as to be depressed. We all experience the latter at some time in our lives, a misery from some easily identifiable cause, which vanishes with the advent of some comforting success or the passage of time.

The inability to organise thought, coupled with physical disturbances such as sleeplessness, constipation, or excessive appetite, and often associated with anxiety of such intensity that it may lead to self-destruction, make up the picture of the affective illness called depressive disease. It may follow mental or physical trauma, such as an injury or a virus infection. Students may develop it after glandular fever and if it persists fail their exams. It can follow childbirth, when it is known as puerperal depression. The underlying mechanism is probably biochemical and in many cases marked improvement can be achieved with anti-depressants, but if the condition is left untreated, it may drag on for years.

The condition is not the prerogative of adults and can occur in children with disastrous effects on their schooling. Because of poor thought organisation, a child finds it impossible to accept even simple new concepts, finds it difficult to express ideas in words or on paper and, in contrast to many other types of learning disability, can make no effort. Typically, spelling shows plenty of rotations ('b' for 'd') of letters at ages when these should not be expected and this type of error can come and go with the depth and severity of the illness. The difference between the performance in the morning and that at afternoon school may be surprisingly marked, and test results would reflect this, to the confusion of teachers trying to place the child in a well-balanced teaching group. Diagnosis and treatment lie in the hands of the child psychiatrist and may well take months. It is vital for the teacher to recognise that though lightening of mood and apparent lessening of misery occur rapidly with treatment, recovery from the underlying thought disorder, and therefore the ability to learn, may take up to a year after treatment has stopped.

Two cases will serve to illustrate the difference between what happens if the condition goes unrecognised and what happens if it is spotted early.

Hazel Neither of Hazel's parents had had any educational problems, though one of them had had a depressive disease at one time. The pregnancy and her birth were normal and she was a placid, easy baby, passing her milestones on time. She did have a congenital abscess at the base of her spine, a common enough condition not associated with learning problems. At the age of seven this was removed by operation. Her schooling was not a success as she had difficulty in learning and was disruptive. Things got so bad that transfer to an ESN school was suggested, but her IQ was found to be low average and therefore too high for such a placement. She attended a remedial teaching centre without benefit and her behaviour and lack of achievement became so unsatisfactory that the local educational authority placed her in a boarding school.

She was thirteen when she was seen at the Clinic, anxious, irritable, sleeping poorly, feeling that no one liked her and thoroughly miserable. Her academic performance was equivalent to that of a seven-year-old at best, and though she was slow in the mornings everyone recognised that she was much brisker in the evenings. She never threatened suicide to adults, but did discuss this possibility with her pets, preferring to confide in her dog rather than in people. In appearance she was tall, with a willowy figure, greasy blond hair and a dress of indeterminate muddy colour. She resented the interview and testing session and laced it with many sighs, sat slumped in the chair, avoided eye contact and if a question was too pressing, shifted herself into an even more accentuated drooping posture. She volunteered nothing, answered with single words. Home was terrible. How terrible? Boring. School, which she had left abruptly half-way through the previous term, had been nasty. How nasty? Boring. The girls had been terrible, the boys she could not remember. Every activity mentioned (cooking, watching TV, listening to records) was dismissed as unwanted, forgotten, or unpleasant. The one exception was riding and grooming a horse.

When reading — very slowly — passages of continuous prose her mistakes were refusals. When reading words of single consonant and vowel blends she confused 'b' and 'd' on 25% of occasions. She achieved no raw score at all in the solo task of silent reading comprehension. Despite rapid and legible cursive handwriting, her spelling ability was comparable to that of a six year-old.

It was suggested that no significant educational progress would be made until she was clinically better, felt more cheerful and was more consistently engaged in something agreeable. Therefore any tuition, which for the immediate future would have to be very low key, should be based on magazines about horsemanship. In due course the basic literacy skills could be tackled through informal games; if and when an improvement was noted, two books for small scale reading and comprehension exercises were suggested: *Read all About It* and *What's This All About?* both by Bill

Ridgway (Edward Arnold). For the time being exercises in spelling and free writing were not to be thought of. Such is the effect of long standing depressive disease.

Hugh Hugh's parents had both suffered from depressive disease at various times and during the pregnancy his mother had been in and out of hospital several times with threatened miscarriages. Before starting school he frequently suffered from throat infections and at the age of six was circumcised. Following this he developed difficulty in going to sleep, and in spite of bright normal intelligence began to slip behind at school. Not only were his reading and spelling said to be below the expected level, but his maths also became noticeably weak, so that he was given remedial tuition in school with little effect. By the time he was 9 years 10 months old things came to a head, with a new maths master trying to introduce him to new working methods. This precipitated a severe depressive illness, which was quickly diagnosed by an alert family doctor and the child psychiatrist prescribed treatment with tablets. Just as this medication was beginning to improve his sleep pattern and lighten his mood, the remedial help in school came to an end. Instead help was arranged for him once a week in hospital. This consisted of physiotherapy to improve his coordination, and speech therapy to improve his slurred articulation and encourage him to sound out words as a way of underpinning spelling. Occupational therapy in the form of painting — which he and his school recognised as one of his strengths — was chosen partly as a means of self-expression, partly to continue developing his obvious talent, and partly because he enjoyed it. Extra time devoted to pleasurable activity improved his spirits. He also had short spells with the remedial teacher. These were at first unproductive because he found it impossible to focus on anything that called for precision.

The breakthrough came three months later over a Christmas present. He had been given a large, versatile and life-like tank. He could not remember what make it represented and it was suggested that if he brought it to the next session the teacher would bring a popular book on armour for Hugh to identify from photographs the make of his tank.

The following week the tank was rapidly identified. The real tank had a maximum speed of X mph. 'How fast does your tank go?' He didn't know. A stop watch was fetched, a length of floor measured and the toy tank put through its paces. By the end of the afternoon's crawling Hugh had established what the maximum speed — in feet per second — of his tank was; if the rate of progress could be maintained how did it compare with the speed of the real tank; what difference to the speed of the toy tank was made by fewer turns of the key, or a 'hill' of a given height and length, or a load of a given weight. While handling the toy Hugh was able to suggest how each mathematical operation should be performed—although, not knowing his tables, he was unable to do the necessary sums.

After that the occupational therapy sessions began to include a reaching element; games of observation were introduced, craft tasks involving the following of printed instructions were added, and finally overtly instructional games for reading and vocabulary were part of his programme. The parallel teacher's sessions were given over to reading for fun (starting with jokes) of material assessed for readability and matched to his rising level of competence. Two months after the tank breakthrough work on spelling was introduced, largely from the *Tutorpack* programme (from Packman Research Ltd, Twyford, Berks) which is fun to handle. Also there was as much conversation as possible about anything of interest: the family boat, a bone found on a beach, a ride on the hovercraft. Sometimes he wrote about a topic of special interest. If this was done at leisure with opportunity to look up spellings, the results were very satisfactory. When hurried his spelling reverted largely to the unorthodox but phonically comprehensible alternatives.

A year later his achievement in reading accuracy, comprehension and speed, as measured by the Neale analysis, were ahead of his chronological age. On entry into his comprehensive school he avoided relegation to the remedial stream, and was justifiably brimming with self confidence—and so performing academically and socially much better than either his parents or teachers had dared hope.

Manic depressives

In adult psychiatry, the alternation of depressive illness with phases of excitement is known as manic depressive disease. There are mood swings from one state to the other, but like the Grand Old Duke of York, there may be periods when the patient is neither up nor down. The disease may occur spontaneously, or as the result of some obvious stress, and is most commonly seen amongst young adults. It does occur amongst children, often starting at an early age around eight or nine and slowly becoming distinguishable from the less complicated depressive illness described in the last section. There are several important points of difference: the miserable child becomes dramatically better, only to rush into overactivity and exuberant, or exhausting, behaviour. Learning does not necessarily follow the change: though the reading performance may improve somewhat during the up swings (spelling stays poor throughout), there is some deterioration during the down swings. So teachers find themselves fostering two slow painstaking steps forward to one step back.

The diagnosis must be made by the child psychiatrist. In our experience treatment makes the behaviour better but does not significantly affect the scholastic performance and the results obtained have always been bad. It is, fortunately, a rare condition. Only seven cases have been seen in ten years in the Clinic.

Harry Harry was referred to the Clinic at the age of ten, because a paediatrician found that he could not spell his name nor read the letter-head saying 'St Thomas' Hospital'. He had had a convulsion when aged six shortly followed by a severe burn. About this time he started to wet his bed and became aggressive and miserable. His reading and spelling had progressed little since the burn. When seen he was humourless, weepy, irritable and slow in the mornings, with marked improvement in the evenings. He could not attempt simple classroom tasks and drew a most miserable picture of himself in profile. Initially he responded well to antidepressant treatment until his mother, judging him to be adequately restored, stopped it. The subsequent mood swings from depression to overactivity took about three months between trough and zenith. At the high points he drew himself full face, with the features of a Smiley, and his reading comprehension would appear to have advanced by elapsed time. In the troughs he reverted to profile self-portraits, showing himself with down-turned mouth, and his reading comprehension measured at well below the previous high. As he got older his mood swings became more marked, and eventually his disruption of group activities, such as class work, became too difficult to contain. Fortunately, with specific medication his behaviour was easily controlled. When last seen at the age of fourteen, he was the star of his local junior football team, but his reading comprehension remained at the level of an eight-year-old and the outlook, at least on the scholastic side, was poor.

Nuisances (hyperkinesis)

Hyperkinesis, hyperactivity, overactivity, poor attention span, inattentiveness, can't concentrate, doesn't concentrate, damned nuisance: the spectrum of description runs from ultra-violet scientific jargon to infra-red angry English. Some definiton is needed.

Hyperkinesis, in Britain, in the paediatric context, refers to persistent overactivity which is apparent under all circumstances. There is no way of holding the child's interest and the lack of attention is so great that no teaching can be done. Hyperkinesis often starts immediately after birth and continues until puberty, when it may be replaced by a contrasting but tolerable passivity. Though sometimes associated with a history of birth trauma, this is not invariably the case. Currently the cause is thought to lie in deficiencies of control exercised by the deep centres of the brain over the level of awareness and reaction to stimulus of the cerebral hemispheres. Incoming messages run riot through the system, instead of being processed in an orderly fashion. This belief is the basis for treating these children with stimulant drugs to increase the activity of the deep centres and consequently improve their control over the cerebral hemispheres. Fortunately these cases are very rare; referral to the child psychiatrist is the only appropriate course.

John John was one of these rare children. After a forceps delivery he was persistently sick and difficult to feed. He was restless and a poor sleeper at all times and was unable to cope with nursery school and infant school. It might be fairer to say that neither nursery nor infant school could cope with him, as he would not sit still, would not sit down, was garrulous and both physically and mentally mercurial. He came to the Clinic at the age of 6 years 7 months, a good-looking, fair-haired little boy, carrying a toy car, a common enough occurrence and one invariably welcomed as offering a topic of conversation. But not in this case. Instead he used it as a pretext for wide arm movements, batting it backwards and forwards between the palms, swinging his body sideways. When he was eventually induced to sit on a chair (having first tried the desk, cupboard and examination couch) he swung his legs, again a common occurrence but not in the size of the arc described by his feet. Tiring of the car he stretched his arms on the table in front of him and swung them round in a large circular motion as if to polish the veneered surface. A moment later, with the car back in rhythmic motion over the table top, the Ballard 60-second mental arithmetic subtraction test was synchronised with the movement and without the least appearance of effort John chalked up a score well ahead of his chronological age. Then he disconnected again. At the case conference the examiners' comments were: 'a very lively boy who gave the impression of quicksilver', 'he gives the impression of a very bright child whose intelligence is grossly unfocused', 'he was a fidgety, distractable little boy who jumped quickly from one subject to another which at times made him sound incoherent', 'tests probably invalid due to lack of attention and distractability.' When all the testers, all the adults, find the child overactive in many different situations, then is the time to consider that there may be true hyperkinesis. Such cases should be referred to the child psychiatrist.

Incidentally the Ballard test (from *Mental Test* by P. B. Ballard, now out of print) was not intended to discover whether he had any idea of number. It was the tester's last attempt — all others having failed – to discover whether his movement could be used towards holding his attention.

Anxiety

Fear and anxiety are normal emotions, useful in small doses, and learning to deal with them is part of growing up. The fears which children experience conform to a developmental pattern and alter with increasing age. At first there is apprehension of tangible and immediate things, like barking dogs and strange men: 'survival now' is what matters. Then imagination takes hold, nasties lurk in the corners of fancy —it is not what can be seen that causes fear, but what is thought to be seen. Between nine and twelve the main worries are about school achievement and what teacher thinks of you. Miss Brodie is in her prime, only to be displaced shortly by concern about self and how to fit in with others, coupled with worries about the future. The next step is that of philosophy and politics and late night introspection over too much coffee.

Fear, the serviceable watchdog of physical safety, loses its virtue when a child finds it difficult to cope with everyday stresses (Rutter and Hersov, 1976). If the foundations of the family are shaky, if there is ill-health from physical or psychiatric disease, or if there are delays in maturation, then normal anxiety may become abnormal. The nervous stomach ache, frequency of micturition or nausea are commonplace, whilst asthma, eczema and migraine become worse in those children who are constitutionally predisposed to them. Behavioural symptoms take the form of attention-seeking, restlessness, poor concentration, forgetfulness, enuresis and sometimes apathy (Frommer, 1972). Learning problems may be both the result or a cause of anxiety. The degree and pattern depend on the nature of the child, his or her age and maternal attitudes. There are many variations on the central theme.

Refusal to go to school may be associated with anxiety. A phobia, an excessive fear, may be sparked off in an otherwise stable child by a sudden mild illness, such as feeling sick in assembly. This sets up a tighter spiral of anxiety in case the same thing happens again in the same circumstances. Some children develop ridiculous rituals to avert the threatened catastrophe: walking in the pavement squares to avoid the bears is and has been normal long before Christopher Robin thought of it, but endless washing and touching is not. Efforts to overcome such phobias may result in hysterical behaviour and apparent paralysis, fits, blindness or other dramatic complaints may suddenly affect the child. Such cases must of course be referred to the physician. His job is to sort out real from imagined illness (though the latter may be as serious as the former); he will be aware that apparently hysterical symptoms may well precede the onset of a physically-based disease.

Charlie Charlie was thirteen when first seen by the Clinic, having been referred by the Eye Department because he could not see the blackboard, but no ocular abnormality was found to account for the functional visual loss. It was thought that he might have a problem in perceiving what he could see. His mother had had some problems in late pregnancy but he was of normal weight on arrival and was a good, easy-to-handle tiny baby, who passed all his milestones at normal times. He got on fine at school until his father died; from then on he became naughty at home, where he was to some extent the man about the house, but he kept up at his school work. The change from primary to secondary school is always a stress; for Charlie it was more than he could cope with. From being conscientious, he became an opter out, but not to the extent of bunking off. Instead he suddenly could not see the blackboard. Yet his long and well-established membership of the school cricket team and attractive legible and rapid cursive handwriting indicated at least visuomotor control above average. He was expansively articulate on his pleasure in all sports (he had a real prospect of making his town's junior cricket team), but much terser on the subject of lessons, especially ones taken by teachers he disliked. Homework, he explained, was set daily and he dispatched it in ten minutes during the lunch hour. This same nonchalance characterised his approach to all the scholastic tests adminstered at the Clinic. He rushed the lot, without bothering to work out by elimination or careful recall the answers to the questions. Guesses were the preferred instantaneous response. The mechanical literacy subskills were well drilled and quite sufficient for coping with all occasions when interpretation of print was unavoidable. Seeing him with his mother, he was subdued and detached from her; she appeared anxious to maintain contact with him and to realign him into cooperation with academic learning.

Caroline Fear of what may happen at home during the child's absence is a potent cause of refusal to go to school. If a threat to the mother is believed to exist, then the child will only be happy as long as she can see that all is well at home; since going to school means not knowing what is happening at home, fear and anxiety take charge.

Caroline was aged thirteen when referred to the Clinic. She had had many events in her history which could have upset her capacity to develop language normally. She was born prematurely and was anaemic for some time after. Before the age of seven she had attacks of ear trouble with periods of deafness. Even so, she coped well with her first experience of school, which for most children is the first experience of leaving home, having to obey strangers and not having parents around for various types of rescue. So Caroline managed well despite being, according to her mother, a nervous child, and she kept up well in class. Unfortunately an irate teacher shook her physically for some misdemeanour and for a short time afterwards she locked herself in the lavatory at home rather than go to school. This was corrected by patience on the part of her parents and school teachers, so that Caroline again went cheerfully to lessons. Some years later a child with whom she was friendly died of leukaemia and then an older woman acquaintance also died. Caroline was sure her mother would follow suit and became aggressive and acutely distressed to the point of drawing a knife on her. Continued daily school attendance was insisted on and achieved only by forceful delivery of the girl through the combined efforts of several adults. This Dickensian pantomime was witnessed daily by her school mates. The picture she presented at the Clinic was interesting and at first glance the expected one: she would not let her mother leave the waiting area while she went to the various therapists' rooms for tests. Her mother complied, going tea-less for the afternoon.

Caroline went through the tests steadily, well able to sustain eye contact and giving brief but adequately informative answers to all questions. These are significant features to distinguish her from depressed children who in the vast majority of cases avoid eye contact and don't know, or don't remember, or just stay silent. She assured the tester that she never sewed, knitted, or did anything with her hands, while her mother assured the doctor that Caroline did knit and make models, with pleasure. She read aloud with much aplomb and her miscues were slight mispronounciations of unfamiliar words and twice sensible admissions, 'I don't know that word.' When answering comprehension questions she gave answers rapidly without intervals for thought. In the silent reading comprehension test her 'mistakes' were only slightly out of context, involving a shift of interpretation rather than misunderstanding or ignorance. Her handwriting was most attractive and efficient, her spelling fully adequate with the miscues being reasonable phonic alternatives. Her school had been giving her part-time teaching with one teacher only for some considerable time.

In contrast to the medical view, the hardpressed class teacher may have a different interpretation of these two cases: two children, both with very anxious mothers, both went through distressing experiences while in junior school. These altered significantly their attitude to learning, but observably learning did not come to a halt. For Charlie at age thirteen had a spelling proficiency equivalent to 12 years 5 months and Caroline's at age thirteen was equivalent to 11 years 10 months. So at least the vagaries of English spelling which arguably require more than plain visual recall had continued to be assimilated. (Incidentally the visual sequential memory of both was very good, in Caroline's case at maximum.) This again is a significant difference from the performance of children suffering from depressive disease. The educationally weakest tested area of both was in comprehension of passages read aloud, that is in answering direct questions. And as school teachers know, alas only too well, if a pupil wants to play dumb this is the traditional slot to do it in. In neither youngster did scholastic performance fall so short of expectation as to render him or her vulnerable in any unavoidable contact with print, and for both their silent reading comprehension (level pegging with chronological age in Charlie's case, and one year behind in Caroline's) were better than many teachers encounter outside remedial streams.

So both children knew enough to get by, both had their mothers at maximum attentiveness, and both had a number of other adults in positions of authority bent on easing their path. The teacher may be forgiven for thinking that Charlie and Caroline were adept at manipulating a series of conscientious and well-meaning adults. The temptation to dismiss the youngsters with a crisp phrase from the robust teacher-pupil vocabulary of seventy years ago must be resisted. For all the medical kerfuffle serves a strictly practical purpose: it offers reassurance and advice to the bemused parent which, if followed, should lead to a calmer stance and more sensible management of the child; and it provides a face-saving framework in which the youngster can evolve out of a pattern of behaviour which has outlived its usefulness.

Clearly both Charlie and Caroline had gone through highly distressing moments and their reactions had been appropriately extreme. These in their turn had evoked adult responses which the youngster had found very acceptable. If continuation of the responses is wanted the behaviour must persist, and will persist until a new element, also acceptable to the youngster, is introduced. Neither the socially inexperienced youngster, nor the parents, befogged by anxiety to the point of lacking all finesse, was able to engineer a way out of the log jam. The psychiatrist, trailing coats of medical scientific magic, could. Therefore the treatment and guidance of such cases lies in the hand of the child and family psychiatrist who is able to unravel the situation.

On the other hand there are cases where unanimity of view will lead to alleviation of anxiety. In these, while home may house the root cause, school will be aware of adding its quota. Particularly prone are children who are asked to tackle academic obstacles beyond their capacity. In such cases adjustment of circumstances may result in relief of anxiety. But if the problem arises because the child has a developmental delay which makes the hurdle that much bigger, then the immediate relief may be spurious and temporary and the whole pattern of trouble may reassert itself to the consternation of child and parents. Just changing the scenery sometimes does the trick, but unless full and proper investigations are carried out the results may be disappointing later. The relationship between anxiety and underachievement, which is not straightforward, is explored by Rutter (1974).

Colin Colin was adopted and had a lot of changes of home and foster parents in his very early life. But he settled down well with his new parents and appeared to be developing normally. Anxious to do the very best for him, his parents sent him at the age of five to an expensive, highly competitive, excellent school. After nine months there he began to wet the bed and was disruptive in class, where everyone else had an IQ in the superior range, which was also the average for the school. Consequently the school's measured average reading proficiency was equivalent to two years ahead of chronological age. Mere age equivalence resulted in remedial tuition three times a week (and excellent tuition at that), and failure to improve led to parents being summoned for a chat with the headmaster. Colin was unable to rise to, let alone maintain, this demanding standard (which, let it be clearly understood, was relished by the able pupils). So with great good sense he refused to cooperate. His forte was to lie on the floor and scream which made it difficult for lessons to proceed. In the Clinic he was found to have a below-average short-term memory, which is often a feature of anxiety, and to have difficulty in accepting a large amount of information unless it was offered in small digestible chunks. He had a minor degree of delay in his language development. Even so, his reading and spelling achievements were within normal limits for his age, with his IQ in the bright normal range, though the verbal part of it was only average. Colin was rescued from his overdemanding environment and went to a school where he was able to cope so that his anxiety was resolved. His language problems remained, but were dealt with on a remedial rather than on a coaching basis. But this happy ending was only possible because, when he had left an independent school, the local authority in Colin's area had a vacancy and could not refuse to take him. This solution is not possible for the child who starts off in a local authority school and on being recommended for transfer cannot be moved because of parental refusal, absence of vacancy, or lack of funding for transfer to an independent school geared to the particular disability. In these instances class teachers are left to cope with the help of such advisory services as may be available in their area.

In the Clinic population failure at school leads to anxiety. The overdemanding aggressive mother is an anxious one: she demands as much attention from the school as her child may be demanding from her. Only recognition and alleviation of the fears which arouse the anxiety will make life easier all round. Easy to say but difficult to put into practice. The well-worn poker-work motto, 'Don't worry, it may never happen', does not apply to the child who fails to read, because it has happened. The familiar bromides, 'He's a slow developer', or 'It will be all right in the end, I'm sure', are of no use in allaying anxiety, any more than is a tranquiliser, which serves only to depress and not to cure.

Anxiety and memory

Memory, a topic with more facets than a fly's eye, has in the Clinic setting a limited range. One particular facet has already been mentioned: a developmental delay in its visual sequential aspect correlates closely with poor spelling, as in the case of Bob (see page 98).

Almost as common, again in the Clinic setting, are children who forget to do what they have been told to do. Sometimes this reaches such proportions that the child is considered wilfully naughty, or else to have a learning disability, in which case he or she is referred to the Clinic. The story is always the same: 'He doesn't remember to do what I tell him to do; he leaves his homework at home, forgets to take it to school (or else he leaves at school something which should have been brought home); he learnt it yesterday but had forgotten it this morning.' The memory task can mean paying attention to something and recalling it later, or the recalling of something not attended to at the time. It can be immediate, short or long-term. Coding systems and processes are implicated, information is reduced to manageable terms and categorised. All these aspects have been apparent in the earlier case histories. A memory problem is sometimes associated with other difficulties of perception and expression, as in the case of Andrea (see pages 54-5). But in a significant number of Clinic cases it is 'pure'.

Anxiety over situations at home or at school are the commonest causes; it seems as if the child hurries to happiness from an impossible situation so intently that all else is forgotten on the way; the dash for refuge from the threatening situation wipes out instructions given. Within the home the dash for refuge may take the form of absorption in a favourite game, endlessly repeated, internal emigration to a private haven. Other causes are psychiatric illness, neurological disturbance, or medicines. Although memory training can be given it is important to remove, if possible, any identifiable cause first; even the most intensive course of Pelmanism will not do any good if the family situation is disintegrating, or the child is repeatedly whacked for not doing the forgotten task. So when a child arrives labelled as 'having a poor memory', a very careful identification of the term is called for, and we try to set about it softly, for often we tread on his dreams.

8
Gifted Children

Readers will have noticed that a large proportion of the children mentioned so far have IQ scores in the bright normal, superior, and very superior ranges as defined by the WISC test. The Clinic does see more of them than the national distribution statistics would warrant, probably because it is so often the court of last resort for children who have puzzled, worried and finally driven up the wall their families and teachers. Is 'giftedness' the root of their difficulties?

Definitions of 'giftedness' vary. In the days of grammar schools, when selection was largely dependent on Verbal IQ as expressed by verbal reasoning tests, a common cut-off figure was 115 or 120. These are the high average children, who if consistently well taught, with support and stimulation at home and steady working habits, should do creditably in academic examinations at the end of their school careers. They are fun and quite easy to teach, as long as no specific difficulty arises to interfere with their physical or emotional development. These are the 'run-of-the-mill gifted'.

The 'severely gifted' are the 2% with IQs above 135. A few have been known to have difficulties attributed to them; for the spanking letter attesting their height of brow includes a rider about the subject's 'low motor speed'. Medical examination shows nothing amiss; conversation reveals that the child is in good time for all necessary activities, that if he happens to oversleep he can dress in five minutes flat (and on cold mornings under the bedclothes, too), that he can run or climb as fast as most of his peers, only his hand-writing is on the slow side. 'But I'm speeding up,' he declares stoutly, and it emerges that he has recently moved from a school where cursive script and writing to dictation were not practised to one where they are, a common enough occurrence in transfer from local authority to independent school. Checking with the school confirms that no problems, motor or otherwise, have been noticed; the staff, who know a very bright lad when they see one, are mildly annoyed by the fuss whilst recognising that parents need reassurance.

Clinic records show parents whose children have moved from a local authority to an independent school to be satisfied with the welcome, time and consideration given to them by the new school and the children to settle down well. Parents are often far more worried by having a child who 'is not like other kids' than by the prospect of mother returning to full time work, sometimes after the age of 40 and years of comfortable housewifery, in order to pay the fees.

The difference from other kids may be an entirely useful one: 'He doesn't scribble on walls and doesn't mess up his toys,' agonised the mother of a six-year-old; sometimes destructive: 'This is the least co-operative, most aggressive, self-willed pupil I have seen in fifteen years,' was one teacher's verdict on a ten-year-old who read perfectly anything to do with aeroplanes or space, refused to utter when faced with any other print, and would not write anything at all. He was transferred to a primary school with a high academic reputation, but his classroom behaviour persisted; in break he chased and larruped the other children, so after a week his parents were asked to remove him. Or the case of Patrick whose headmistress wrote, 'We are at the end of our tether with him. Since he entered this school at the age of five he has not paid the slightest attention in class, he rushes through everything and then starts playing and distracting the other children.' Yet his reading and spelling proficiency were way ahead of his seven years, his handwriting beautiful, his tasks completed in neat exercise books full of well-observed illustrations, he tackled mechanical three-dimensional jigsaws with speed and success, and was most observant of adults' speech patterns. All to no avail, for the school asked the parents to remove him. They happened to live in a country district, with no other local authority school within reasonable travelling distance. However, his father had a modest mortgage, there were only two children in the family, so the parents were able to pay school fees and Patrick to benefit and enjoy the more intensive tuition and new intellectual tempo of his independent school.

Some families veer towards the independent sector. In other cases, after consultation with the support service, the child — after a period of home tuition organised by the Education Authority — is transferred to another school more suited to his predominant need. Subtler forms of pressure can be exerted on children whose IQ and achievement are consistently high, whose behaviour gives no real cause for complaint, but who somehow fall foul of their teachers. These have been known to pick on some minor aspect of performance, generally handwriting, and complain about it so vehemently that at the age of transfer to secondary school the crucial gradings and appraisals are distorted by this one minor point. Parents try hard to be reasonable: 'He does seem to us like a bright boy and we wouldn't like him to be penalised for poor presentation. Can something be done to help him? You see in our district there's now only one school with a good A stream.' Help with poor handwriting is offered, an electro-encephalogram may be indicated, but more often all that is necessary is the charitable view teachers happily extend to average pupils.

Briefly, gifted children have two hurdles to cross: rapport with their teachers, and the ability of the school to provide them with the stretching they require. The first can be immediately troublesome. Some teachers have difficulty in accepting a pupil whose performance is so different from the average and their own. Charity is hard to maintain in the face of a child who consistently gets through all tasks faster and better than everybody else and then entertains himself, at best by demanding further stimulation from the teachers, or more often by inventing activities which are fascinating to his class mates. His oracy, reading and general knowledge are likely to be a long way ahead of his peers, he may seem endlessly energetic, with great interest in all things mechanical, a tenacity in pursuing a subject, lynx-eyed observation and delighted response to new ideas. Complex directions and prolonged working on his own will be taken in his stride. He is likely to exhaust all adults and most children.

The head of the school, at a distance from which generosity of spirit is easier to maintain, will have the practical problem of catering for the tiny minority of severely gifted children. What resources has he for them, what else can he lay hands on to help them, how much more time can he devote to them? For with all their independent habits these children are not satisfied with one minute of adult attention a few times during the school day — they clamour for fifteen minutes concentrated attention. The temptation to say 'Let them get on with it, they'll be all right' is very powerful, especially in the context of a school covering the whole spectrum of ability and with no banding.

There are of course, benevolent schools, perceptive teachers, sensible parents, and the gifted child in their midst is still not catered for as one would wish. Nine-year-old Peter was one of them, an extremely high and seemingly effortless performer in a highpowered school, where despite everybody's encouragement and kindness he was observably not happy. His mother's anxiety about him brought them to the Clinic. He was very self-possessed, had a delightful slow smile it took hard work to elicit, and sustained a well-informed conversation about the camps on the Roman Wall, accounting for the architectural features that differentiated the two infantry camps from the cavalry one. This led easily to sculpture and it transpired that, though art was his best and favourite subject, his school unfortunately had scope for only painting and drawing. He was longing to come to grips and be shown how to tackle tie-dying, silk-screen printing, weaving, clay, stone and constructional sculpture in metal, and so on. But, he added, he sometimes had trouble with maths, and it would be nice to sort it out. The Clinic suggested that a school with large grounds, where he could play or daydream should be sought — a school which would also give ample opportunity for all art-based work and careful maths teaching. There was no difficulty in finding one that filled this specification and the transfer was effected with good will on all sides.

Some children who turn out to be consistent high fliers come to the

Clinic almost as an afterthought. They have been prodded by conscientious teachers to have a small niggle investigated just before O-levels. It is always a residual spelling difficulty. What to do at such short notice? They are advised to learn the spelling rules and directed to *Logical Spelling* by B.V. Allen (Collins), which lends itself to working on one's own; or to seek out an old-fashioned junior school teacher who will, in a few sessions at week-ends and in the Easter holidays, put them through accelerated spelling drill. If this is too expensive, parents are asked to dictate passages from leading articles, book reviews, modern novels, and every time a mistake is made to try to explain it: that is, if 'thinner' is spelt with one 'n' write it out correctly and follow with copying out the doubling rule; or if the auditory approach is preferred, spell it out loud and say the rule on to a tape. These spelling tapes can be played at odd moments in the run up to the English O-level, and as soon as it is over the whole palaver can be thankfully forgotten. In this context it is worth examining carefully the English language O-level papers of the various boards. They vary considerably and two, relying on multiple choice for comprehension questions, make life easier for the shaky speller.

When youngsters at this stage of their schooling come to the Clinic, conversation always turns to the sequel: what A-levels are you thinking of taking? Looking through the records one 100% correlation emerges: the youngsters who confidently face A-levels in English and history speak warmly of the friendship, understanding, humour and close support of their arts subject teachers. This is not to suggest that maths and science teachers are a set of curmudgeonly Herods. Experience points to the precise opposite! But on the limited evidence available, the high flier with the slight problem will take to English or history only as a result of considerable and very sensitive support from his teachers.

'Giftedness' therefore implies a high IQ, consistently maintained through the eleven years of compulsory schooling, combined with high performance in the academic or creative fields or both. Intellectual curiosity, well-established hobbies covering a wide range of interests, extensive general knowledge, ability to work without supervision, originality and inventiveness, speed of problem solving, an unusually wide vocabulary are some of the characteristics which are just as significant as the children's academic divergence from the norm. They all need generous enabling adults to bring out their surprising potential. And the adult's life is a lot easier if the gifted are also good humoured, modest and considerate.

This is seldom the case with the flawed ones, children with high measured IQs who for a variety of reasons (often emotional ones) are nowhere near attaining their potential. Even with patient and devoted help their progress is puzzlingly slow, and each one of them progresses in a different way, calling for the most observant and versatile teaching. They need a book on their own, for they are like Snaug's treasure, first glimpsed by Bilbo Baggins, needing the concerned efforts of hobbit and lake dwellers to bring it to light and to useful purpose.

At the time of going to press three developments are having an impact on the management of gifted children in local authority schools. The Schools Council have published 'enrichment packages' covering a limited number of subjects; the package on drawing and painting is particularly attractive. The present government's assisted places scheme, enabling children to transfer to the independent sector, will bring appropriate education to a very limited number of gifted chldren. The change-over from selective to comprehensive education is almost complete and has brought into sharp focus the problem of the isolated gifted child especially that of the isolated gifted child from an ethnic minority.

9
Conclusion

At the end of the day, when the child has been observed, tested, examined, discussed, reported on, the reports integrated into recommendation, how much good does the Clinic do?

With so many different types of case this question is not answered briefly. There is a spectrum of achievement running from obvious success to just as obvious failure — at one end the cases which we know we are going to make better and do, and at the other end the cases that we view with what turns out to be justifiable foreboding.

When a firm medical diagnosis can be made early in the child's school life, and if the disease is one which admits of treatment, then the outlook is good. Clinical conditions may not have been diagnosed outside the hospital, either because a full assessment was not available locally and the medical condition became hidden under a more obvious behavioural problem; or for social reasons (such as change of home, or non-attendance at school medical service) as a result of which the child had managed to slip through the net.

The early diagnosis and treatment of depressive disease by the Child Psychiatric Department can solve the learning disability which was merely a symptom of it. Children are seen who are partially deaf or are partially sighted, either of which can result in an apparently intelligent child underachieving at school work. It is characteristic of both conditions that the pupil/patient invariably sits at the back of the class, or as far away from the teacher or blackboard as possible. Adjustment of epilepsy therapy, recognition of petit mal or temporal lobe attacks, so mild that they have escaped detection, or of such recent onset that they have come to the hospital for diagnosis, result in improvement if not in cure. Relief of anxiety — that is, anxiety of sufficient intensity to require the services of a child psychiatrist — will also show dividends. In the same category comes the curtailing by the Clinic of over-expectancy on the part of adults dealing with the child. The child of normal intelligence in a high-powered school, or in a high-powered family, may be regarded as a failure when compared to sisters, parents, or rivals in the classroom. Not all of us are born brilliant and in some cases parents and schools are equally to blame for expecting too much from an ordinary child and thereby making him extra-ordinary. The same applies to the low average child, well taught and willing, who falls short of what everyone expects. If the true situation can be recognised by all the adults, the relief is enormous and the swan that was rapidly turning into a goose becomes a swan once again, though perhaps in a smaller pond.

Success depends on accurate diagnosis. What about failure?

The fourteen- or fifteen-year-old with a persistent history of school failure, an understandable history of poor attendance, a low average IQ and a reading age of no practical use in the world after school is, from the strictly academic point of view, a poor prospect. But life goes on after school and holds the hope of providing the motivation which is lacking in the school setting — money. Not only the necessity of eating, but also the pleasure in receiving cash for effort can transform the situation for the 'non-achiever'. Pound notes are as valuable in restoring self-confidence as are swimming badges or a tick at the bottom of an exercise book with 'better' written alongside. Close co-operation with the Careers Service and the Colleges of Further Education can result in an improved situation. Later, when morale has also improved, or the girl friend has persuaded him, the non-reader may come to Adult Literacy Classes for help. These too require the services of assessment units, for they too may fail unless adequate investigation of the possible cause and type of reading failure has been carried out.

It is difficult to determine to what degree the job hunter is handicapped by illiteracy. Some firms ask all applicants for work to fill in details of health and past employment on a form, the personnel officer leaving the aspirant alone in an office to do this. Strategies for dealing with this unmanageable situation vary from 'Left my glasses at home' to downright flight. (Other firms test reading levels even for apparently manual work and will reject applicants if they do not pass.) Others actively recruit poor readers, recognising that they may have skills and talents, other than reading ability, which are valuable. Unfortunately enlightened firms are difficult to find. The non-reader is in danger of being at the bottom of the employment pile, and however intelligent he may be, finds that the only employment open to him is dangerous, dull and dirty. There is an obvious temptation to resort to crime rather than struggle unsuccessfully in a society that does not seem to value what the illiterate has to offer.

There is a high correlation between delinquency and school failure, both during school years and afterwards. The Home Office Research Unit Report on thirteen-year-old Approved School boys, *The Approved School Experience* (1962), found that though the boys had a slightly lower intelligence than would be expected, there was a significant retardation in reading and the older they were the more striking this was. The extent to which future crime can be prevented by adequate reading teaching has not, as far as we know, ever been defined. There is a story, perhaps apocryphal, that young men who received remedial teaching in prison would commit crimes on discharge in order to attend the classes once more.

Between the poles of Clinic success and Clinic failure lie the bulk of the patients. Their conditions are not clearly definable in medical terms. Attached to them are all sorts of labels describing symptoms without defining the underlying brain mechanisms, because nobody knows what they are. As Defoe describes in his *Journal of the Plague Year,* when the cause of a condition is not known some people run about the streets with repeated cries of 'Lord have mercy upon us. What shall we do?' and others write *Abracadabra* on bits of paper. So it seems now with learning problems. Dysphasia, dyslexia, dysgraphia, hyperkinesis, hyperactivity, maladjustment, brain dysfunction, the words are legion. So what does the Clinic do?

At the basic level of courtesy and communication everybody concerned with the child is informed of the Clinic's findings. The parents are invited for a private discussion with the doctor during which a full explanation of the results obtained is given, together with any information required about what the tests test, and how the Clinic interprets the findings. To withhold information from the parents is to assume that responsibility for action lies in the hands of the teacher or doctor, but it is the parents who must decide on the course to take, the Clinic staff being in an advisory role. Generally parents are very receptive of Clinic advice, the discussions are genuinely fruitful exchanges of views and it is possible to map out at least in outline ways of management and treatment that will improve the child's behaviour and learning. The instances in which this understanding is not achieved are fortunately very rare. There was one memorable occasion, with the cause of trouble clear and the remediation reliable and readily available, when the father (a lawyer) in particular argued back volubly and vehemently. Absolutely not one vestige of consensus was achieved, and the departing parents 'cast out their shoe over Edom'. A chastened case conference was re-convened, the same conclusion as before was arrived at. But there was no way of initiating remediation because the parents had not given permission for Clinic findings to be passed on and the parental right to confidentiality is always rigorously observed.

However, the vast majority of parents accept the diagnosis offered and realise that an improvement can seldom be achieved by the family acting in isolation. So the child's school teachers are very often invited to contact the Clinic and sometimes they visit or telephone. Copies of the Clinic's final summary and the teacher's recommendations are sent to all concerned parties. This places a load on the Clinic secretary but is clearly responsible for much of the satisfaction patients and their mentors derive. The foundations are, at least theoretically, laid for a cooperative effort to get the child learning by the most suitable steps.

A large intractable group consists of underachievers in whom the accumulation of several strands of slight disability cause learning delays and leave the class teacher uncertain where to begin. The teacher probably has a well-defined image of the 'normal' child and the quality and quantity of his response to educational stimuli, but is unable to get the pupil to this level of 'normal' development. The Clinic, by establishing each individual child's 'norm' at a particular moment in his development, offers advice on the strengths to be worked through and the weaknesses to be strengthened or circumvented. But some aspects of a child's development may not be susceptible of improvement even in the long term. For instance, a disability in fine visuo-motor coordination may make it impossible ever to write a rapid and legible hand in adequate quantity under stress conditions. Some cases take so long to come right that learning programmes are thrown out of kilter. This particularly applies in cases of depressive illness, which if unrecognised can cause a learning delay representing several years of school work. Similarly a delay in the maturation of visual sequential memory — which appears strongly to influence spelling proficiency — to an age when spelling is no longer routinely taught, may well deprive the youngster of that easy command of the written word essential for academic success. Several of the learning deficits caused by poor development of oral language are remediable so far, and then – unless backed by a transformation of the family's linguistic style — no further. Leaving aside the vexed definitions of semi-literacy and literacy, all remedial teachers know that it is easy for pupils to achieve a reading (and sometimes also spelling) proficiency equivalent to that of an eight- to nine-year-old. A number of carefully structured programmes based on a variety of approaches lead thus far. Each successful method is equally valid; the skill consists in selecting the one, or parts of several, most suitable to the child. The crunch comes at the next stage when in face of inadequate further oral language development reading progress also flags. At this stage programmes are much thinner on the ground and teachers are thrown back on their own resources, with the immense richness of the vocabulary, the conflicting demands of various subjects, the constraints of group teaching making the task brutally complicated and tending to fragmentation. The imperfect theoretical basis of much remedial tuition and the lack of information as to which method achieves which end was ably described by Yule in 1976, when writing about the issues and problems in remedial education.

It must be clearly understood that, in the authors' view, it is no part of a hospital's job to usurp the functions of the educational authorities. Except in the narrow field of medicine and its ancillary services, a hospital is not a classroom. But it can diagnose and treat and therefore the true worth of a Clinic lies in the provision of services not readily available outside the hospital.

The problem for both the Clinic and the educational authorities is that definite labels cannot be attached to a large number of learning difficulties, because of a lack of basic scientific knowlege necessary for accurate diagnosis and the subsequent genuinely successful treatment. Much research remains to be done, but not by a diagnostic clinic which by its nature is a service unit. We carry on trying to sort out the treatable from the teachable and passing on the results of our investigations to parents, schools and family physicians. For far too many children this is far too little.

Epilogue

The remedial teacher, having read through this book, may justifiably feel restive: everything so far confirms classroom experience; a single clear-cut reason for a particular child's failure in school is not often identified amongst the Clinic's cases; most of the children have many adverse events in their histories, both medical and social, which could be held accountable for the presenting symptoms and picture. The investigations at the medical, psychological and educational levels serve to point the way for therapy and educational techniques. But what specific guidance, backed by evidence, is offered without quibbling?

Fortunately there are some well-defined cases where specific treatment in a limited field produces results. It is consequently tempting to assume that only one cause is responsible and the removal of that cause accounts for the success obtained. To be certain that *post hoc ergo propter hoc* really holds good in these cases, detailed epidemiological studies of whole populations are necessary, and these are quite beyond the scope of a hospital clinic. The best that can be produced as evidence is a series of anecdotes related by similarities. But anecdotes are the froth from which research ideas may spring, like Aphrodite from the fecund sea, so the authors make no apology for the results obtained from three different patient clusters, which have in common moderately successful outcomes following treatment.

Investigation of a clinic case is like peeling an onion or opening a Chinese box, only to find another layer or another box inside the first — depending on how deep you delve and when you are prepared to stop, the more you are likely to find out. At the initial assessment only three layers are explored: medical, psychological and educational. The three clusters under consideration represent work at those levels, the first two of which may have a direct bearing on the last.

Patients sufferng from depressive disease (pages 104-7), poor speech sound discrimination (pages 48-51), or who are tinkling cymbals (pages 65-9) have been selected as representing the impact of medication, speech therapy, or remedial teacher recommendation on the reading comprehension of the appropriate cluster. Of course, being able to understand what one reads is not the be-all and end-all of the Clinic's activities, but behaviour, happiness, misery and even handwriting are difficult to quantify. On the other hand the Neale test results can be clearly defined and provide a rough index of success of failure.

Depressive disease

Amongst the last 250 patients who have returned for follow-up, 35 were diagnosed as suffering from depressive disease by the Child Psychiatric Department, whose responsibility it was to supervise drug treatment. The results obtained with 23 children who attended for follow-up after taking anti-depressant medicine are shown in Table 1, whilst the results obtained in twelve children who attended for follow-up when not under treatment are shown in Table 2.

Seventeen of 23 treated cases showed a true gain in their Neale reading comprehension age compared to chronological age.

One of the twelve untreated cases showed a gain in reading comprehension age compared to chronological age, whilst the reading age of another had kept pace with time elapsed. The other ten showed true losses.

These figures may seem convincing, superficially, but it must be remembered that many other factors could be important: age, sex, intelligence, teaching techniques, changes in family dynamics — all would have to be considered to make the figures meaningful. Tables 1 and 2 are offered only as anecdotal evidence that appropriate treatment should be taken into account when reviewing the achievements of children suffering from depressive disease.

Table 1
Depressive disease — cases treated with antidepressive drugs

Case number	Sex	IQ	Age in months at time of exam	Neale reading comprehension age in months	Gap reading comprehension age in months
1	M	average	81	nil score	N/D
			94	88	
			105	106	
2	M	bright	83	87	N/D
		normal	94	104	
3	M	average	92	78	
			126	113	122
4	M	bright	103	80	N/D
		normal	115	94	
5	M	average	110	84	N/D
			115	106	
6	M	bright	113	nil score	N/D
		normal	133	90	

Table 1 continued

Case number	Sex	IQ	Age in months at time of exam	Neale reading comprehension age in months	Gap reading comprehension age in months
7	M	low average	113	nil score	N/D
			123	nil score	
			137	nil score	
8	M	average	115	nil score	N/D
			139	101	
9	M	bright normal	118	106	N/D
			124	125	
			131	128	
10	F	average	119	103	N/D
			132	121	
11	F	average	122	104	N/D
			130	115	
12	M	bright normal	123	149	
			157	147	196
13	M	bright normal	126	121	N/D
			133	147	
14	M	superior	130	98	N/D
			140	98	
15	M	average	130	78	N/D
			139	98	
16	M	average	133	98	102
			173	151	161
17	M	bright normal	134	111	
			162	109	145
18	F	low average	135	78	N/D
			141	94	
19	M	bright normal	136	98	N/D
			144	111	
			153	136	
20	M	average	138	107	
			166	114	90
21	M	average	142	106	N/D
			156	125	
22	M	average	151	81	68
			167	94	93
23	M	bright normal	152	94	
			170	149	126

Table 2
Depressive disease — cases not treated with antidepressants

Case	Sex	IQ	Age in months at time of exam	Neale reading comprehension age in months	Gap reading comprehension age in months
A	M	average	85 118	nil score 90	N/D
B	M	average	94 100	104 101	N/D
C	M	average	105 133 145	90 107 107	N/D
D	M	average	114 142	90 106	N/D
E	M	bright normal	118 136	80 98	N/D
F	M	bright normal	126 130	92 98	N/D
G	M	average	143 151	87 81	73 68
H	M	average	146 179	125 138	N/D
I	M	low average	147 153	101 94	N/D
J	M	average	150 160	133 109	N/D
K	M	low average	161 177	98 98	N/D
L	M	not done	161 169 216	80 81 101	N/D

Speech sound discrimination

Poor speech sound discrimination is identified by the speech therapist and its correction is her interest. She is not directly concerned with teaching reading or writing, but rather with the creation of language adequate for the child's use in school. Her efforts are directed at improving oracy and she is most effective with younger children.

Amongst 150 children under eleven who returned for follow-up, eleven were found to have poor speech sound discrimination and normal hearing. The results obtained from the application of the therapist's advice are shown in Table 3 (see below). Included in this are the number of errors in speech sound discrimination made by each child at each testing. In all eleven cases there was an improvement in this capability and a concomitant increase in comprehension of the spoken word. Three of the four youngest children showed a net improvement in reading comprehension. But it seems that the older the child at the time of initial examination, the greater the persistent discrepancy between chronological and reading comprehension ages. In other words, it is probable that the sooner children with speech sound discrimination problems obtain help from the speech therapist the better.

Table 3
Poor speech sound discrimination

Case number	Sex	IQ	Age in months at time of exam	Neale reading comprehension age in months	Errors in speech sound discrimination (out of 30)
1	M	dull	83	nil score	8
		normal	92	77	3
2	M	bright	95	78	8
		normal	100	90	3
3	F	low	96	83	10
		average	108	87	5
4	M	superior	98	90	8
			106	101	3
5	F	bright	105	95	5
		normal	117	101	0
6	M	average	108	90	5
			119	90	3
7	M	average	114	101	10
			128	106	3
8	M	bright	115	90	10
		normal	127	100	4
9	M	bright	122	90	14
		normal	142	109	0
10	M	low	127	81	10
		average	134	81	5
11	M	low	130	90	6
		average	138	88	1

Tinkling cymbals

If the doctor or the speech therapist is treating a patient, he has to return to the hospital if he wants to go on being cared for. The remedial teacher's recommendations are implemented at school so that return to the Clinic is not essential. This means that when recommendations have led to success there may be no follow-up examination; the suggestion that the child come again for reassessment produces not the patient but a letter from the school or parent saying that now she or he is better there is really no point in another visit. For this reason the number of tinkling cymbals that have been seen a second time is low. Table 4 (see below) details the results obtained in nine cases from amongst the 150 who returned for follow-up recently. It shows the striking difference between the Neale accuracy scores and the Neale comprehension ones, and that, when the

Table 4
Tinkling cymbals — those cases for whom the remedial teacher's recommendations were implemented are marked with an asterisk*

Case number	Sex	IQ	Age at exam in months	Neale reading accuracy ages in months	Neale reading comprehension ages in months	Gap reading comprehension age in months
1	F	borderline	92	72	nil score	N/D
			106	78	nil score	
2	F	low average	106	94	87	N/D
			174	144	118	
3	M	average	120	nil score	nil score	N/D
			143	106	80	
4	M	bright normal	130	152	113	N/D
			145	147	114	
5*	M	average	131	135	109	N/D
			136	134	128	
6*	F	bright normal	146	137	125	
			159	138	140	
			170	147	146	170
7*	F	superior	159	143	103	
			170	146	131	202
8*	F	bright normal	166	144	130	
			173	147	134	
			215	N/D	N/D	191
9*	M	average	177	143	107	118
			204	121	98	above ceiling

recommendations outlined in a previous chapter (pages 65-9) are implemented, good results may be expected. Older children of fifteen or more are best tested with the Gapadol rather than the Neale, so that results obtained with cases 8 and 9 have to be seen in this light. The excellent results obtained serve to emphasise the importance of not teaching reading as an automatic skill but to ensure that what is read is understood.

A last cautionary tale

He was first seen when aged 8 years 3 months. He was of superior intelligence. Though his reading was almost two years in advance of his chronological age he never read for fun, and his spelling was distinctly poor. He was disinclined to co-operate and his most frequent reaction to questions and requests for change of activity was, 'I don't know,' or 'I can't,' and a sag of the shoulders.

The Clinic was not alone in observing such a picture. At school, where he often reverted to babyish language, he was in need of constant reassurance. Despite much extra help he had great difficulty in producing written work, and his spelling remained stubbornly resistant to remedial efforts. If homework included any writing he just screamed.

A number of possible courses were considered. Perhaps something had happened at his birth; perhaps his mother was over-anxious and over-protective; perhaps there were tensions at home; perhaps he had not been taught in the, for him, most appropriate way: all the usual perhapses — none with any real foundation. What to do, when you don't know the answer? Bring him back in about a year to re-assess the position.

He came back in ten months. The findings this time were important enough to warrant describing him on his own. His school reported that he was now a keen reader, and his form teacher had hopes that he might win a scholarship. The Clinic staff found him to be forthcoming and loquacious, full of ideas. He was a new boy. His reading comprehension was more than three years ahead of chronological age, his spelling about half a year behind. The change had been wrought, not by the Clinic, nor by the school, but by the Ear, Nose and Throat surgeon who had taken out his chronically infected tonsils. Which does not mean that every unco-operative child should lose his tonsils, but is rather a warning that general illness can affect performance as much as anything else.

Medical Bibliography

ABERCROMBIE, M. L. J. (1964) *Perceptual Visuo-motor Disorders in Cerebral Palsy.* London: Heinemann Medical.

ALBERS, R. W., SIEGEL, G. J., KATZMAN, R. and AGRANOFF, B. W. (1972) *Basic Neurochemistry.* Boston, Mass.: Little, Brown.

ANNEL, A.-L. (1972) 'Depressive states in childhood and adolescence', in *Proceedings* of the Fourth UEP Congress. Stockholm: Almqvist and Wiksell.

AYRES, A. J. (1973) *Sensory Integration and Learning Disorders.* Los Angeles, Calif.: Western Psychological Services.

BADDELEY, A. D. (1976) *The Psychology of Memory.* New York: Basic Books.

BARLOW, H. B. (1975) 'Visual experience and cortical development'. *Nature,* 258: 199-204.

BERRY, M. F. (1969) *Language Disorders of Children.* New York: Appleton-Century-Crofts.

BRADLEY, L. (1980) *Assessing Reading Difficulties.* London: Macmillan Education.

CASHELL, G. T. and DURRAN, I. M. (1971) *Handbook of Orthoptic Principles.* Harlow: Longman.

CONNELL, H. M. (1979) *Essentials of Child Psychiatry.* Oxford: Blackwell.

CRYSTAL, D., FLETCHER, P. and GARMAN, M. (1976) *The Grammatical Analysis of Language Disability.* London: Edward Arnold.

CYTRYN, L. and McKNEW, D. H. (1972) 'Proposed classification of childhood depression'. *American Journal of Psychology,* 129: 149-55.

DAVIDSON, H. P. (1935) 'A study of confusing letters B D P and Q'. *Journal of Genetic Psychology,* 47: 458.

DAVIS, R., BUTLER, N. and GOLDSTEIN, H. (1972) *From Birth to Seven.* Harlow: Longman.

de la CRUZ, F. F., FOX. B. H. and ROBERTS, R. H. (1973) *Minimal Brain Dysfunction.* New York: New York Academy of Sciences.

FAIRBANK, A. (1961) *A Handwriting Manual.* London: Faber.

FINUCCI, J. M., GUTHRIE, J. T., CHILDS, A. L., ABBEY, H. and CHILDS, B. (1976) 'Genetics of specific reading disabilities'. *Annals of Human Genetics,* 40: 1-23.

FROMMER, E. A. (1968) 'Depressive illness in childhood', in COPPEN, A. and WALK, A. (eds) *Recent Developments in Affective Disorders.* London: British Journal of Psychiatry Special Publication No. 2, RMPA.

FROMMER, E. A. (1972) *Diagnosis and Treatment in Clinical Child Psychiatry.* London: Heinemann Medical.

GARDINER, P., MacKEITH, R. and SMITH, V. (1969) *Aspects of Developmental and Paediatric Ophthalmology.* London: Heinemann Medical.

GOLDBERG, H. K. and SCHIFFMAN, G. B. (1972) *Dyslexia: Problems of Reading Disabilities.* New York: Grune and Stratton.

GRAY, H. (1977 n.e.) *Anatomy: Descriptive and Surgical.* PICKERING, P. and HOWDEN, L. (eds) New York: Crown (Bounty Books).

HOLLON, T. H. (1970) 'Poor performance as a sympton of masked depression in children and adolescents'. *American Journal of Psychotherapy,* 1972: 258-68.

HOWE, M. J. A. (1975) *Learning in Infants and Young Children.* London: Macmillan.

HUNT, J. and MacAUSLAN, A. (1979) 'Eurythmy and reading disabilities'. *Remedial Education,* 14: 12-13.

HYDE, D. M. G. (1970) *Piaget and Conceptual Development.* New York: Holt, Rinehart and Winston.

ILG, F. L. and AMES, L. B. (1975) *Child Behaviour.* New York: Dell.

INGRAM, T. T. S. (1963) 'Chronic brain syndromes in childhood other than cerebral palsy, epilepsy and mental deficiency', in MacKEITH, R. and BAX, M. (eds) *Minimal Cerebral Dysfunction.* London: Heinemann Medical.

JOHNSON, D. J. and MYKLEBUST, H. R. (1967) *Learning Disabilities.* New York: Grune and Stratton.

KALVERBOER, A. F., van PRAAG, H. M. and MENDLEWICZ, J. (1978) *Minimal Brain Dysfunction: Fact or Fiction?* Basle: Karger.

KEPHART, N. C. (1971) *The Slow Learner in the Classroom.* Columbus, Ohio: Charles E. Merrill.

KNOBLOCH, H. and PASAMANICK, B. (1959) 'Syndrome of minimal cerebral damage in infancy'. *American Medical Association: Journal,* 170, 12: 1384-7.

LASHLEY, K. S. (1963) *Brain Mechanisms and Intelligence.* New York: Dover.

LEVINE, M. D. and LIDEN, C. B. (1976) 'Food for inefficient thought'. *Pediatrics,* 58, 2: 145-8.

LINNETT, M. J. (1976) 'People with epilepsy — the burden of epilepsy', in LAIDLAW, J. and RICHENS, A. (eds) *A Textbook of Epilepsy.* Edinburgh: Churchill Livingstone.

LEVINSON, H. N. (1980) *A Solution to the Riddle Dyslexia.* New York, Heidelberg, Berlin: Springer Verlag.

LUNZER, E. A. and GARDNER, K. (1979) *The Effective Use of Reading.* London: Heinemann Educational.

LURIA, A. R. (1973) *The Working Brain.* Harmondsworth: Penguin Books.

MacAUSLAN, A. and QUIN, V. (1976) 'The rotation of confusable letters in the writing of depressed children'. *Child: Care, health and development,* 2: 379-86.

McCARTHY, J. J. and OLSON, J. L. (1964) *Validity Studies on the Illinois Test of Psycholinguistic Abilities.* Madison, Wisc.: University of Wisconsin.

McFIE, J. (1975) *Assessment of Organic Intellectual Impairment.* London: Academic Press.

MacKEITH, R. (1963) 'Defining the concept of minimal brain damage', in MacKEITH, R. and BAX, M. (eds) *Minimal Cerebral Dysfunction.* London:

Heinemann Medical.

MARTIN, J. A. M. (1972) 'Hearing loss and hearing behaviour', in RUTTER, M. and MARTIN, J. A. M. (eds) *The Child with Delayed Speech.* London: Heinemann Medical.

MENKES, J. H. (1974) *Textbook of Child Neurology.* Philadelphia, Pa.: Lea and Febiger.

MICHELL, G. (1963) 'Notes on the so-called "minimal brain damage" syndrome with particular reference to family dynamics', in MacKEITH, R. and BAX, M. (eds) *Minimal Cerebral Dysfunction.* London: Heinemann Medical.

MITTLER, P. J. (1970) *The Psychological Assessment of Mental and Physical Handicap.* London: Methuen.

MURRAY, P. A. (1970) 'The clinical picture of depression in school children'. *Irish Medical Journal,* 63: 53-6.

MYKLEBUST, H. R. (1963) *Development and Disorders of Written Language,* Vol. 1. New York: Grune and Stratton.

NAIDOO, S. (1972) *Specific Dyslexia.* Report of the ICAA Word Blind Centre. London: Pitman.

NELINGER, G. A., KOLVIN, I., SCOTT, D. M. and GARSIDE, R. F. (1976) *Born Too Soon or Born Too Small.* London: Heinemann Medical.

NEWTON, M. (1977) *Dyslexia: Recognising the Phenomenon.* London: British Dyslexia Association.

OPPE, T. E. (1969) 'Risk register for babies'. *Developmental Medicine and Child Neurology,* 9: 13-21.

PAGE, S. and MacAUSLAN, A. (1978) 'Poor handwriting and the pencil hold in learning disabled children'. *British Journal of Occupational Therapy,* 41: 252.

PASAMANICK, B. and KNOBLOCH, H. (1966) 'Retrospective studies on the epidemiology of reproductive causality: old and new'. *Merrill-Palmer Quarterly of Behavior and Development,* 12: 7-26.

PENFIELD, W. and ROBERTS, L. (1959) *Speech and Brain Mechanisms.* Princeton, N.J.: Princeton University Press.

PETERS, M. L. (1975) *Diagnostic and Remedial Spelling Manual,* London; Macmillan Educational.

PIAGET, J. and INHELDER, B. (1956) *The Child's Conception of Space.* London: Routledge and Kegan Paul.

PIAGET, J. (1959) *The Language and Thought of the Child.* London: Routledge and Kegan Paul.

QUIN, V. and PASCALL, P. (1978) 'Copying and spelling skills'. *British Journal of Occupational Therapy,* 41: 398-400.

QUIN, V. (1979) *Reading Games.* Malvern: Cressrelles.

RICHARDSON, G. (1974) 'The Cartesian frame of reference. A structure unifying the description of dyslexia'. *Journal of Psycholinguistic Research,* 3, 1:15-63.

RICHARDSON, M. (1935) *Writing and Writing Patterns: teacher's book.* London: Hodder and Stoughton.

RUSHWORTH, G. (1963) 'A physiologist on the cerebellum', in WALSH, G. (ed.) *Cerebellar Posture and Cerebral Palsy.* London: Heinemann Medical.

RUTTER, M., GRAHAM, P. and YULE, W. (1970) *A Neuropsychiatric Study in Childhood.* London: Heinemann Medical.

RUTTER, M., TIZARD, J. and WHITMORE, K. (1970) *Education, Health and Behaviour.* London: Longman.

RUTTER, M. (1974) 'Emotional disorder and educational underachievement'. *Archives of Diseases in Childhood,* 49: 249-56.

RUTTER, M. and YULE, W. (1975) 'Concept of specific reading retardation'. *Journal of Child Psychiatry,* 16: 181-97.

RUTTER, M. and HERSOV., L. (1976) *Child Psychiatry.* Oxford: Blackwell.

SANDBERG, S. T., RUTTER, M. and TAYLOR, E. (1978) 'Hyperkinetic disorder in psychiatric clinic attenders'. *Developmental Medicine and Child Neurology,* 3: 20.

SANDERS, D. A. (1977) *Auditory Perception of Speech.* Englewood Cliffs, N.J.: Prentice-Hall.

SHERIDAN, M.D. (1962) 'Infants at risk of handicapping conditions'. *Monthly Bulletin* of the Ministry of Health, 21: 238.

SHERIDAN, M. D. (1964) 'Development of auditory attention and language symbols in young children', in RENFREW, C. and MURPHY, K. (eds) *The Child who Does not Talk.* London: Heinemann Medical.

SLOAN, W. (1955) 'The Lincoln Oseretsky motor development scale'. *Genetic Psychology Monograph,* 51: 183-252.

SMITH, P. (1977) *Developing Handwriting.* London: Macmillan Educational.

TARNOPOL, L. (1969) *Learning Disabilities.* Springfield, Ill.: Charles C. Thomas.

TAYLOR, I. G. (1964) *The Neurological Mechanisms of Hearing and Speech in Children.* Manchester: Manchester University Press.

TOOLAN, J. M. (1962) 'Depression in children and adolescents'. *American Journal of Orthopsychiatry,* 32: 404-15.

TOWBIN, A. (1971) 'Organic causes of minimal brain dysfunction'. *American Medical Association: Journal,* 217, 9: 1207-14.

WIIG, E. A. (1976) 'Language disabilities of adolescents: implications for diagnosis and remediation'. *British Journal of Disorders of Communication,* 11: 3-17.

YULE, W. (1967) 'Predicting reading ages on Neale's Analysis of Reading Ability'. *British Journal of Educational Psychology,* 37: 252-5.

YULE, W. (1976) 'Issues and problems in Remedial Education'. *Developmental Medicine and Child Neurology,* 18: 674-82.

Tests Bibliography

BRIMER, M.A. and DUNN, L.M. (1962 [Tests 1 and 2] and 1970 [Test 3] *English Picture Vocabulary Tests.* Bristol: Educational Evaluation Enterprises (distributors).

CARVER, C. (1970) *Word Recognition Test.* London: Hodder and Stoughton.

ELLIOTT, C. D., MURRAY, D. J. and PEARSON, L. S. (1978) *British Ability Scales.* Windsor: National Foundation for Educational Research.

FROSTIG, M. *et al.* (1964) *Frostig Developmental Test of Visual Perception.* Palo Alto, Calif.: Consulting Psychologists Press; Windsor: National Foundation for Educational Research (distributors).

KIRK, S. A., McCARTHY, J. J. and KIRK, W. D. (1968) *Illinois Test of Psycholinguistic Ability.* Champaign, Ill.: University of Illinois Press; Windsor: National Foundation for Educational Research.

McLEOD, J. and ATKINSON, J. (1972) *Domain Phonic Tests.* Edinburgh: Oliver and Boyd.

McLEOD, J. and UNWIN, D. (1970) *GAP Reading Comprehension Test.* London: Heinemann Educational.

McLEOD, J. and ANDERSON, J. (1973) *GAPADOL Reading Comprehension Test.* London: Heinemann Educational.

NEALE, M. A. (1957-8) *Neale Analysis of Reading Ability.* London: Macmillan.

PETERS, M. L. (1975) 'Peters Diagnostic Dictations', in *Diagnostic and Remedial Spelling Manual.* London: Macmillan.

SCHONELL, F. J. and SCHONELL, F. E. (1960) 'Schonell Spelling Test', in *Diagnostic and Attainment Testing* (4th ed.). Edinburgh: Oliver and Boyd.

WECHSLER, D. (1949) *Wechsler Intelligence Scale for Children.* New York: Psychological Corporation (Harcourt Brace, Jovanovich); Windsor: National Foundation for Educational Research (distributors).

WEPMAN, J. M. (1958) *Auditory Discrimination Test.* Chicago, Ill.: Language Research Associates.

YOUNG, D. (1964; 3rd ed. 1978) *Non-Readers Intelligence Test.* London: Hodder and Stoughton.

YOUNG, D. (1973) *Oral Verbal Intelligence Test.* London: Hodder and Stoughton.

YOUNG, D. (1976) *SPAR (Spelling and Reading) Tests.* London: Hodder and Stoughton.

Publishers' and other addresses

Edward Arnold (Publishers) Ltd, 41 Bedford Square, London, WC1B 3DQ.
E. J. Arnold and Son Ltd, Butterley Street, Leeds, LS10 1AX.
A. and C. Black (Publishers) Ltd, 35 Bedford Row, London, WC1R 4JH.
William Collins Sons and Co. Ltd., PO Box, Glasgow, G4 ONB.
Cressrelles Publishing Co. Ltd, Little King's Hill, Wallwyn Road, Upper Colwall, Malvern, WR13 6PL.
Peter Daffon Associates, 30 Marsh Road, Pinner, HA5 5MQ.
Department of Prices and Consumer Protection, Millbank Tower, Millbank, London, SW1P 4QU.
Educational Evaluation Enterprises, 5 Marsh Street, Bristol, BS1 4AE.
Galt Toys, Brookfield Road, Cheadle, Cheshire, SK8 2PN.
Hamleys of Regent Street Ltd, 200 Regent Street, London, W1.
George G. Harrap and Co. Ltd, 19-23 Ludgate Hill, London EC4M 7PD.
Heinemann Educational Books Ltd, 22 Bedford Square, London, WC1B 3HH.
Hodder and Stoughton Ltd, PO Box 6, Mill Road, Dunton Green, Sevenoaks, Kent, TN13 2XX.
Hutchinson Educational Ltd, 24 Highbury Crescent, London, N5 1RX.
I L E A Learning Materials Service, Highbury Station Road, London, N1 1SB.
Learning Development Aids, Park Works, Norwich Road, Wisbech, Cambridgeshire, PE13 2AX
Longman Group Ltd, Longman House, Burnt Mill, Harlow, Essex, CM20 2JE.
Macmillan Publishers Ltd, Houndmills Estate, Basingstoke, Hants.
Thomas Nelson and Sons Ltd, Nelson House, Mayfield Road, Walton-on-Thames, Surrey, KT12 5PL.
Oliver and Boyd, Robert Stevenson House, 1-3 Baxter's Place, Leith Walk, Edinburgh, EH1 3BB.
Oxford University Press, Walton Street, Oxford, OX2 6DP.
Penguin Books Ltd, Bath Road, Harmondsworth, Middx, UB7 ODA.
Philip and Tacey Ltd, North Way, Andover, Hants, SP10 5BA.
Remedial Supply Co., Dixon Street, Wolverhampton, West Midlands.
Taskmaster Ltd, Morris Road, Leicester, LE2 6BR.

Index

Index of Case Histories